HODDESDON HIGH STREET
A Nostalgia Trip

Stephen Jeffery-Poulter

2014

HODDESDON HIGH STREET:
A NOSTALGIA TRIP

Copyright © Stephen Jeffery-Poulter 2014

ALL RIGHTS RESERVED

NO PART OF THIS BOOK MAY BE REPRODUCED IN ANY FORM,
BY PHOTOCOPYING OR BY ANY ELECTRONIC OR MECHANICAL MEANS,
INCLUDING INFORMATION STORAGE OR RETRIEVAL SYSTEMS,
WITHOUT PERMISSION IN WRITING FROM BOTH THE COPYRIGHT
OWNER AND THE PUBLISHER OF THIS BOOK.

9781908616746

First Published 2014 by
Berforts Information Press

Printed and bound in Great Britain by
Berforts Information Press
www.bookprinting.co.uk

ACKNOWLEDGEMENTS

I'm extremely grateful to all the local residents who I approached or who came forward voluntarily for giving up their time to share their stories and experiences of the town which form the backbone of my narrative. They are all recorded in the Contributors List at the back of the book. Of course, I'd never have heard these wonderful anecdotes unless Steve Fisher had agreed to work with me as Director on the two documentaries we made together on the history of Hoddesdon in 2011 and 2012.

Phil Oldridge, Information Services Librarian, East Area for Hertfordshire Library Service, once again was kind enough to give me access to Hoddesdon Library's Local Studies Collection and made various enquiries and searches for me. David Dent was, as ever, enormously supportive and generously loaned me his extensive collection of postcards, photographs and other ephemera – including some very rare examples of shop receipts which appear in this book.

I have been very fortunate to have benefitted from the work of all the previous historians who have written about the history of Hoddesdon before me: A J Tregelles in 1908; H F Hayllar in 1948; David Dent in 1992 and Sue Garside in 2002. However, the person I feel most beholden to is Edward Paddick, not just for his book *Tales of a Hertfordshire Town* published in 1971, but for the enormous amount of research he undertook over the forty or more years following his appointment as the town's first Librarian which is now tucked away in the bowels of Hoddesdon Library. Furthermore, the documents, images, artefacts and ephemera which he collected so assiduously for most of his life paved the way for the creation of Lowewood Museum a few years after his death. In addition, he was at the forefront of many campaigns through the 1960s and 70s to save the heritage of the town which he so loved.

With regard to the illustrations - I am indebted to Tommy Knight for giving me permission to use a selection from the many thousands of photos and adverts featured in the Hoddesdon Journal which his company published for over three decades. I have George Don to thank for the use of a wonderful range of pictures he has taken over many years, along with other photos of the town he has collected. And I would like to express my appreciation for the material from their photo albums and personal collections which many of the interviewees have generously loaned for inclusion, to Phil Carter and Peter Lardi for the use of their family pictures and cuttings, and also to Bryan Smith for letting me feature his exclusive photos of the Morrisons construction project. All the illustrations, of course, remain the copyright of the various owners. Whilst I have made every effort to contact copyright holders of any additional material I apologise in advance for any omissions and invite those people to contact me so that their work can be acknowledged and/or removed from future editions.

Last but by no means least I have to thank my partner Alan without whom this project would never have been completed.

This book is dedicated to the memory of our shop dog Miss Ellie, who was not only a wonderful pet but a special companion for nearly a decade. She was much loved and will always be greatly missed.

INTRODUCTION

Welcome to my 'virtual tour' of Hoddesdon Town Centre – over the next 200 pages we're going to make our way north along the west side of the High Street, cross to the other side and walk back in a southerly direction. As we stroll along I'll be telling you the history of each of the buildings we encounter – the properties that preceded them on the site, the individuals and families who have lived and worked there, and the different businesses they housed over the centuries. We'll also take a few detours down certain side streets so as not to miss some key buildings. I am using this approach to reveal the town's history, as it has already proved to be extremely popular as the basis for a series of talks I've given to local groups over the last 18 months.

Piecing together those stories has been as a result of a considerable amount of research – reading past histories of the town; consulting articles in various editions of the monthly *Hoddesdon Journal* which was published between 1935 and 1967 as well as looking at the adverts they carried over the decades for the local businesses; and carefully studying the numerous period photos of the town. However, what my book contains for the first time is the personal memories and anecdotes from nearly two dozen retired local residents talking about what it was like to grow up, live and work in their town between the 1920s and 1970s.

Although I have only had the pleasure of knowing Hoddesdon for just under a decade I have really enjoyed learning about its long and interesting history, initially from the local customers who stopped by to share their stories of the town in the past. After working with local historians David Dent and Sue Garside on the book *'Hoddesdon & Broxbourne Though Time'* in 2010 the number of people coming to talk to me increased exponentially and I felt it was vitally important to find a way to record and share those precious but ephemeral memories.

This provided the impetus for me to revive my former programme-making skills in partnership with local corporate video director Steve Fisher to produce two documentaries about the town's past: *Hoddesdon: History & Heritage* in 2011 and *Hoddesdon: In Living Memory* in 2012. The latter, in particular, was packed with extracts from interviews with elderly people talking about their lives – as one of our oldest interviewees, Arthur Wingate, put it to me *"Well, I suppose people of my age are living history."*

And, of course, he is so right – and in this book I'm really pleased to have been able to include a lot more of the reminiscences that those people were kind enough to share. The uncut interviews have been deposited on DVD in the Local History Collection at Hoddesdon Library for anyone who wants to view them in full, now or in the future. In addition you will also find a lot of new material from interviews of others who have volunteered to chat about their experiences for this specific project.

In 1963 Mr Snellgrove, a local surveyor, was commissioned by Hoddesdon Council to produce a report on the Town Centre, just prior to the Tower Centre re-development. He commissioned a set of black and white photos from local photographer Bishop Marshall of every single building in the High Street. We are therefore extremely lucky to have a unique record of what businesses or shops were located in each property at this single moment in time, just before the forces of change swept so many of them away. Therefore, for convenience, as we progress on our journey I shall be identifying each location by the trader who was in residence in 1963.

I apologise in advance for any errors - and there will probably be a few - as personal recollections do fade over time and individual accounts can contradict each other. Also, prior to the Second World War, many traders did not bother to include their addresses in their publicity as this was an age when shopping locally was the norm; shops moved locations and changed their names over the decades, and the town included a variety of stores which shared the same names, despite the fact that the owners were not necessarily related. In 1935 there are three retailers named Bryants, four Nicholls, and two called Norris.

HODDESDON HIGH STREET:
A NOSTALGIA TRIP

And so we start our excursion at the south end of the town on the west side of the road at what is one of the least glamorous and apparently uninteresting locations in the town: the Shell Petrol Station

HODDESDON MOTOR COMPANY (21, High Street) currently Shell Petrol Station and Unique Citroen.

In the 1920s this was the Golden Lion Garage owned by Frank Turner, conveniently located as weary travellers arrived on the first leg of their journey north out of London. According to an advert in 1924 they offered *Motor Cars For Hire: Experienced Drivers. Stabling Accommodation, Horses taken in at Livery.* By the early 1940s the business is still under the same ownership, but had been re-branded as Frank Turner's Car Mart - the local dealer for Vauxhall, Austin and Morris models.

However, by the mid 1950s the garage was being run by R F Hollman who operated the petrol station, repair workshop and car showroom under a new name: the Hoddesdon Motor Company. Obviously business must have been booming by 1965 as a major re-development was carried out - Sherbourne House to the south was purchased and demolished allowing for a virtual doubling in size of the site. Today the only original building to survive is the on-site shop which previously served as the car showroom.

Hoddesdon Motor Company (1963)

THE GOLDEN LION (23, High Street) still the Golden Lion

One of the town's four remaining ancient inns, tradition says Henry VIII saddled his horse here and went out to hunt wild boar. The 'king's saddle' which belonged to the monarch was kept here for centuries and is supposedly now displayed in a bar at Niagara Falls in New York State, although google searches have so far failed to verify this. However, an early tenant of the Salisbury further up the High Street *(see page 71)* was a former servant of that king, so it is just possible there may be a grain of truth in the tale.

The hostelry first appears in local records in 1591 by its former name the White Hinde due to the fact it's tenant, a widow Locke, was being prosecuted for not having a proper licence for selling 'wittlinge' meaning 'victuals' - or what we'd term pub grub. At this time the property was owned by the Rawdon family who lived opposite in their grand mansion.

According to the Herts Session Rolls of 1595-6, opening hours of inns were severely restricted: *"None of them shall suffer any person or persons whatsoever (except suche as shall lodge within the house) to tarry within his house after nyne of the clock from Easter Daie until Michelmas; nor after eight of the clock in the winter."* All landlords in the 16th century would have brewed their own ale on the premises. But another contemporary licensing rule stated: *"None of them shall sell any ale or bear above the rates of four pence a gallon and that every one of them shall have a second sorte of ale and bear which they shall sell for tuppence a gallon."*

By 1756 the tavern had acquired its present name and shortly afterwards must have benefitted, as did all the town's hostelries, from the enormous increase in carriage traffic during the coaching era. Today there is a very interesting staircase just inside to right of main entrance which leads up to a dead end. It is thought there was originally another door half way up the front wall of the building to enable passengers to disembark from the upper part of the coaches straight into the inn. At the rear there was an outside staircase which went up to the Ostlers Room and, until the 1950s, an old mounting block used by coach passengers was kept in the back yard. As late as 1860 there were still a staggering 36 inns and 5 beerhouses in Hoddesdon. In 1896 Henry T Griffin is listed as landlord of the business.

By the 1960s Peter Mawson was the licensee, as Les Riches remembers: *"He was a round-faced man, jolly man. We used to ride our motorbikes from Rye Park up there on a Tuesday night and have a pork pie and a pint, play darts and that sort of thing."* Peter Haynes was another regular:

Sherbourne House, Hoddesdon Motor Company, Golden Lion (1963)

"My favourite pub in those days, and still is in some ways, the Golden Lion – I was one of the Golden Lion crowd. In those days, of course, it had two very separate bars: it had the public bar and the saloon bar. I was a public bar boy and we used to go in there and have our Rum & Coke and those sorts of things. We used to have great fun in there."

AN ACCIDENT OF GEOGRAPHY

Just as it is not a co-incidence that these two businesses - one catering for the transport requirements of travellers and the other to their hospitality - are found adjacent to each other, I have deliberately chosen to start our tour here because they provide the key clues as to how and why the town grew up in its current location and prospered for 500 or more years.

We find the first written record of a settlement here in 'Hodesdone' in the Domesday Book of 1086 which lists the various manors owning land, livestock and rights. As the remains of the old Roman Road Ermine Street to the west of the town began to disintegrate, the 'Old North Road' from London moved eastwards down into the Lea Valley when a new bridge was built at Ware in the late 12th century diverting travellers away from the more dangerous ford at Hertford. Hoddesdon, situated at a crucial junction on one of the main roads, became established as a stopping place for travellers heading for Newmarket and Cambridge to the east or on northwards to York.

In his book Tregelles describes what the town probably looked like in the mid 13th century. *"The hamlet then consisted of something under 50 houses scattered thinly along both sides of the high road beginning at the top of Spital Hill; a farmhouse where Yew House stands paying a rent of 'one red rose and a gillyflower'; another farmhouse, probably Hogges original Manor House... an inn where the Congregational Chapel stands; the market cross opposite the end of Lords Lane... the Maidenhead site was open land; a manor house with dovecote and grange stood a little way down facing this space; a spring rose close to the corner opposite the brewery and overflowed down Stanstead Valley."*

By the 15th century the principal traffic through the town would have been cattle drovers with their herds en route to the expanding Capital. The meads around Tottenham were used as grazing for herds on their way to market from the north.

Given the importance of the route through the town, Hoddesdon has seen more than its fair share of Royal visitors. Edward I must have passed by on his way to his northern capital at York. Later Mary Tudor would have been seen en route to and from her father's house at Hunsdon, as would her younger sister Elizabeth I who also frequently visited her cousin Sir Henry Cary at Hunsdon and Courtier, Sir Ralph Sadlier, at his grand home in Standon. James I's Royal Progress from Scotland to London to take the throne must have been an extraordinary spectacle for the townsfolk, and we know the King was entertained royally on 6th May 1603 at Broxbournebury by Sir Henry Cock. The monarch later persuaded his first minister Robert Cecil to hand over his father's magnificent Theobalds Palace at Cheshunt as a 'gift', and subsequently must have been spotted regularly riding through the town heading to Royston where he had a Hunting Lodge.

His son Charles I, who also used Theobalds Palace, would have marched up and back to Scotland through our nearby hamlet during the Civil War, as would his nemesis Oliver Cromwell en route to his Cambridgeshire home. During the same period Izaak Walton, author of classic fishing and philosophy book *The Complete Angler* published in 1653, regularly walked out of London to practice the art of piscator in the rivers and streams of the Lea Valley. He and his fishermen friends used the popular Thatched House Inn here in Hoddesdon as their base, which is described as *"famous for ales and cakes"*. According to Tregelles:" *In Pepys day our road, bad as it was, seems have been preferred to the other, for he records in his famous diary, in May 1668, travelling from Bishops Stortford to Bishopsgate 'by a privy way which brought us to Hoddesdon, avoiding the bad way of the forest.'"*

Charles II travelled by same 'privy way' as his loyal servant to get to Newmarket for regular race meetings. In 1683, on one of these regular trips, a group of plotters planned to use a lonely and narrow stretch of road adjacent to Rye House to ambush and kill both the king and his hugely unpopular brother and heir to the throne, James. Historians are now somewhat suspicious about how far the Rye House Plot had really developed before one of the conspirators allegedly confessed, giving Charles II a convenient excuse to round up a group of courtiers and disaffected aristocrats who opposed his brother's succession and have them imprisoned or executed.

COACHING DAYS

Hoddesdon was one of many places which became coaching towns during the heyday of the stage coaches in the late 18th and early 19th century. From the 1750s onwards with the establishment of local Turnpike Trusts the quality of roads in Britain began to improve funded by a system of tolls. By the late 18th century Hoddesdon had three toll gates, the oldest near Rye House to the east, another at Fourways just to the north, and a third to the south near Spital Brook.

This drastic upgrading of the nation's highways led in turn to an exponential increase in carriage traffic - which received a further significant boost in 1784 when the Royal Mail started their stage coach services to improve the speed and efficiency of deliveries. Over the next 50 years the country enjoyed the fastest and most efficient form of public transport the world had ever seen. In his book Edward Paddick describes the scene: *"In those last years of the coaching era, Hoddesdon was a bustling little market town with a population of just less than 2,000; thirty one coaches – of which four were mail coaches – came to, or passed through it daily, and one can perhaps picture the hustle and bustle as the guard's horn heralded the approach of a coach."*

By 1835 the earliest coach arrived in Hoddesdon at 7.45am, with the latest leaving at 6pm. The sight of dozens of these brightly painted, elegant coaches pulled by teams of four or six sweating horses speeding along the wide High Street with their horns blaring, disgorging post and passengers while ostlers hurried out with fresh replacement horses must have made the town a busy place. The Bull Inn offered an early breakfast for travellers who had stayed there overnight and wanted to leave on the first coach north to Cambridge. It had stabling for 45 horses, while the Salisbury Arms and Golden Lion could both accommodate around two dozen. In addition there were many packhorses carrying goods through the town and the Vine Inn just off Amwell Street had stabling available for them too.

In the Domesday Book 49 people, mostly bondsmen and villeins, are mentioned by name, suggesting Hoddesdon had a population of just 130. By the middle of 16th century there seem to have been around 650 residents, which gradually increased to 1000 by 1750. The first official census of 1811 recorded 227 houses with 1227 inhabitants. By the end of the century there were over 1000 dwellings and 4781 residents. When the enlarged Urban District was formed in 1935 it had a population of 10,560.

WILLIAMS BROTHERS (25, High Street) currently Saffron Indian Restaurant

The first building we encounter as we stroll northwards up the High Street was built in 1934 on the former site of 'The Laurels' – a grand Georgian mansion of three stories dating to the 1760s. Paddick explains: *"By the 1880s it had become the home of Mr William Frogley, one of three farming brothers, each of whom had a farm in the district. Cows were kept at the rear of the building, but as there was no entry from the High Street, cows and farm vehicles made their entry by way of Brocket Road and along the backs of the buildings in the High Street."* Apparently there was a wooden lean-to on the south end of the house which sold flowers, plant pots, wedding bouquets and wreaths as well as supplying milk in jugs or metal cans.

The new property is split into three separate units, the first of which was a traditional grocers shop called Williams Brothers. Personal service was the norm in the first half of the twentieth century – assistants stood behind long counters with the groceries stored or displayed on their side. As the customer went through their shopping list the staff then fetched and carried items to place in that person's shopping basket. George Don recalls: *"They used to measure you a pound of sugar into a blue bag and used to fold the top up – came out of a sack, they used to scoop it out. Cheese – it was on ration then - there was a wire and they used to just chop off what you wanted."*

Les Riches' mother took him shopping there too, attracted by an early form of loyalty scheme which the shop operated. *"They used to have these, what my mum used to call 'cheques'. They were tin tokens, if you like. You'd go to this cash booth and they used to reckon up how much you owed. You used to pay your money and they would give you these tokens which were like a dividend, and they were worth varying amounts of money. And they were gold and silver, but just stamped out of bits of tin with an oval 'Williams Brothers' logo on them. And depending on how much you spent, you got the value in these tokens that you could save up to exchange at Christmas or whenever to take a bigger discount off your big shop."*

WOOLWORTHS (25A, High Street) currently Bed-e-Buys

Dear old 'Woolies', sadly now consigned to retail history, was one of the town's most popular shops and one of only a handful of national chains represented in Hoddesdon until well into the 1960s. Initially known as the '3d and 6d store', according to Joan Umney, *"they sold everything under the sun, did Woolworths."* Les Riches remembers purchasing light bulbs in the store. *"Where they used to buy the light bulbs, they weren't like they are now - packaged up in nice cardboard boxes. They were just stood on top of the counter. So you'd say 'I'll have a 100 watt bulb', and they'd take it and plug it in and test it. It just had an open-circuit tester – just a bayonet holder. They'd just put it in and if it lit up it was yours – it was a good bulb."*

The spacious store with a noisy wooden floor and numerous long counters stuffed with all sorts of goods was as popular with children as their parents and, hardly surprisingly, many retired residents have fond memories of the place. Annette Marples told me: *"For sweeties, you used to tell someone behind the counter what you wanted, two or three of this and that, make it up to a quarter pound, or two ounces, or whatever it was we wanted. They used to have big boxes of broken biscuits, so you used to get quite an assortment, some bits were little tiny bits, but other bits were quite big."*

Williams Brothers, Woolworth & Co, and Timothy Whites (late 1950s)

Diana Borchards (formerly Diana French) recalls: *"At the sweet counter the assistants had little white caps. The shop floor was a bit waxy and covered with what looked liked sawdust - probably to stop people slipping. My friend also had to buy for her mother 'Californian Poppy' scent imported from America, which wasn't common then. She said it smelt awful, and was horribly strong."*

TIMOTHY WHITES (25B) currently Taste of China Restaurant

The final section of this property was occupied by a branch of the national chain of chemists from the 1930s to the late 1960s.

GIBSONS + HOME & COLONIAL (27A + 27B High Street) currently Antony Davies Lettings and Marys of Enfield

Originally a menswear shop run by Mr Barker Marsh whom Edward Paddick remembers for *"his many eccentricities."* Later this property housed two adjacent retailers: a greengrocers run by the Gibson family and a branch of another store chain called Home and Colonial, which Neville Townsend describes as *"a rather fusty grocers."* Joan Umney reminisces: *"They had big counters with marble tops for the cheeses and the butter which I think was cut with wires and they had spatulas. I used to do that when I worked in a shop, as well. And the staff wore uniforms*

South-west end of the High Street showing Norris' Drapers on the extreme left (c1900)

and hats as well – I think they were white. Everything was weighed up in front of you. And they had those big tills with the large keys that went 'ker-ching'."

Les Riches had a family connection with one of the senior staff. *"Mr Putt was the manager of the Home & Colonial and his wife actually ran the shop when he was in the forces during the war. When he came back from the forces he then resumed as manager of the shop – my cousin married his son."*

The town centre was only bombed once during the entire Second World War - on the night of 10th May 1941 fourteen bombs fell in a line to the west of the town centre. Several shops at the south end of the High Street were badly damaged – including Gibsons and the Home & Colonial Stores. Mary Young witnessed the scene shortly after the raid: *"Gibsons were bombed out – because when we came out from the Catholic School, we came out of Esdaile Lane across the crossing there, and it was all fenced round and that's where the crater was where the bomb dropped. My mother knew Mrs Gibson – she used to do a lot of dressmaking and that kind of thing. You couldn't get things like bananas, but because she worked for Mrs Gibson we ended up getting things like that."*

In the aftermath of the bombing Gibson's re-located further up the street, but the Home & Colonial had its premises hastily rebuilt – a new frontage hid the fact that the rest of the premises consisted of a large Nissen hut. These corrugated metal structures were being manufactured in enormous quantities at this time in a large factory just outside the town at Rye House. This 'temporary' repair lasted another 50 years, until the property was re-developed towards the end of the 1980s.

INTERNATIONAL STORES + BAXTERS BUTCHER (29 + 31, High Street) currently Pizza Hut and Marconato Restaurant

This was previously the home of builder, William Hampton, who ran a sawmill and workshops at the rear of his house in a large glass-fronted building three stories high which, Hayllar writes in his book, *"provided myself when a boy, together with others of my own age, with a fine playground, as we used to run all over the old mill playing hide and seek – not always to the proprietor's relish."* Businesses clearly had no Health & Safety Executive to worry about in those days!

In the early years of the twentieth century it housed a greengrocer called Smiths, before becoming the town's branch of another grocery chain in 1908, International Stores. Neville Townsend's family shopped there during the war. *"International was the place we were 'registered' with for* rationed items. We had a weekly delivery which came in a cardboard box. I rather think my Mother had a monthly account - there was a small cash book listing the purchases and the costs. As a child I was fascinated that our ration included 4ozs of marge, so we had half an 8oz packet!" By the early 1960s the southerly third of the store has been sub-let to a branch of Baxter's chain of butcher's shops and by 1967 International Stores were gone.

ALLEN'S (31, High Street) currently Li's Chinese Takeaway

From the turn of the 20th century this narrow premises was used as a 'cycle and wireless store' run by Mr Allen offering *'BSA: The Best Name in British Bicycles'* in 1936. A new bike would cost from £3 19/6d which could be paid off at two shillings (10p) a week. By 1939, although still stocking tricycles and 'pedal kars', they had become a toy shop offering *'Soft Toys, Trains, Forts, Soldiers, Garages and Model Cars, Model Aeroplanes and Ships for Construction'*. In addition they also sold gramophone records.

By the early 1960s this building had become the home of a small gift shop called Meeks; by the 1980s Elizabeth's Florists had moved here from their former premises at number 41A.

NORRIS DRAPERS (33, High Street) currently Hoddesdon Express & Delight Cafe

The first drapers shop was established here by Mr Lock in 1834 – originally there was a tenement on this site dating back to at least 1530 when it was called Sharnbrooks, which later changed to Sherbornes; the present building replaced it about 1860. The first Mr Lock played a key role in town affairs in the latter part of 19th century, he helped to raise funding for the Congregational Church and was one of the founders of the Hoddesdon Gas Co.

His son Edward W Lock, (known as 'Teddy' Lock), took over the business in 1867 and ran it as 'linen draper and outfitter' until shortly before his death at the age of 90. He was one of the original members of the new Hoddesdon Urban District Council. He was also the first person to lay stone paving outside his shop – the rest of the High Street didn't get pavements until 1902. Paddick tells us: *"He is best remembered for his interest in Hoddesdon Market and for his being responsible for the planting of the holly hedge in what is now known as 'Holly Walk'."*

Mr and Mrs Norris who had just got married became the new owners in 1902 and were in residence for nearly half a century. Through the 1930s their monthly adverts in the *Journal* were jaunty and full of humour. A 1935 advert featured a poem promoting 'Jantzen' swimwear:

August we greet thee
So warm and so gay
So much less of work
And far more of play

So we'll swim every time
We can possibly fix
And buy three suits each
And look 'up to dick'.

If only your length
Was as long as our whim
Our Jantzens would surely
Be getting too thin.

Their annual sixteen day Summer Sale in July included '*frocks, millinery, undies, swim suits, prints, linens, household goods, hosiery, gloves, etc.*' This was a typical example of the wide variety of products sold by stores in the past. In some cases these were not always closely related to each other – the other shop run by an unrelated Norris family in Amwell Street sold motorbikes alongside radios and televisions!

Dorothy Chilton was a regular customer. *"Mr Norris was lovely – he used to more or less welcome you into the shop. I remember him as a very gentle person with white hair; he often would be near the door and open it for you. He wore a country style, tweedy suit. You went straight in and there was an open area – to one side there were bales of material and cloth, the other side was haberdashery. You went up a staircase and that was all hats and dresses and corsetry and everything for ladies. You had an assistant come to help you - Mrs. Street, formerly Miss King, served you up there – and she would bring hats and so on over to you to try this and try that – you were served properly."*

One thing that many of my interviewees remember vividly as children was the shop's high tech payment system. Neville Townsend went there to get his uniform for St Francis School which was in a big house at the end of Brocket Road run by Miss Lawson. *"You had to pay the shop assistant at the separate desk or the section appropriate to your purchase, and then she would put the money in a sort of purse that would go by an overhead cable to the cashier who would then return a receipt and any change by the same process."*

Although their shop was damaged by the bombing raid in May 1941 they carried on regardless – as their regular monthly advert in the Journal announced *"BLITZED – but BUSY. Stock undamaged and we are very much at your service."* Interestingly, this was the only oblique reference in the *Hoddesdon Journal* to the bombing – probably since the

BLITZED but BUSY

STOCK undamaged and here we are very much at your Service.

The Prudent folk are quietly getting on with their buyings, because a time of scarcity is surely at hand. "Quotaitis" has a very disconcerting effect on one's habits. So get your favourite colour while you can. If impossible—Well—laugh at habit and have a real change over and it may be surprising what a thrill you will get. We are doing our utmost to keep as well stocked as possible. So call and give us a look before you say—It just can't be done.

Maybe it can—at

W. S. NORRIS
33 HIGH STREET, HODDESDON
Telephone: Hoddesdon 2140

Advert in the Hoddesdon Journal (1941)

Government restricted this sort of information, partly due to its impact on civilian morale and also as they didn't want the Germans to know how successful or accurate their raids had been. As the war progressed the store's regular *Journal* adverts became much more sober, making helpful comments and practical suggestions about rationing, the blackout and shortages. Looking back these really embody the plucky 'carry on and make the best of it' spirit of the British people as things got increasingly tough on the home front as the conflict dragged on.

The family's second son, Gregory Norris, had joined the army in 1940 and initially served in North Africa as a tank gunner before being sent to Italy where he contracted Malaria and was invalided out in 1942, spending the next 2 years in hospital. In 1945 the *Journal* reported on his early death at only 37 years old, leaving a widow and two young children, adding *"He was always of cheerful disposition and very popular in the town."*

In February 1946 further tragedy struck, with the Hoddesdon Journal reporting the sudden death of both Mr and Mrs Norris within a few days of each other. *"Although he suffered a grievous loss only a few months*

William Stanford Norris (1946) Gregory Norris (1945)

ago in the death of his son Gregory... Mr Norris had carried on in his usual cheerful manner so that his death came as a great shock to his wide circle of friends. He was at his business as usual on Tuesday, but collapsed on Wednesday and died at his home." The 74 year old draper's wife then collapsed shortly after his funeral and remained unconscious until her own death five days later.

By the mid 1950s shop had been taken over and was being run by Mr Nuttall, with assistance from his wife Delphine, daughter Monica and son David. Their monthly *Journal* adverts became more colourful and reflected a wide range of promotions establishing them at the heart of their local community, such as their annual *'happiest baby competition'*. Hedley Eariss tells the amusing tale of the role that the store played in his own origins: *"My mother had this fixation about green; the colour green was her colour... And as far as we know from family history, one day, they had a green pram in there. So, the green pram had to be brought, and I had to be born because she'd got to have the green pram."*

By the 1980s the shop was called Ashleys and consisted of a pharmacy on the left hand side and a glass and china section to the right. By the end of last century it had been split into two separate units with Ashley's Gifts on the south end and the Delight Coffee and Sandwich Bar next door.

HAYLLAR & SON CHEMISTS (35 High Street) currently Flames Takeaway

This next grand and imposing building containing three separate premises was erected on the site of what was described in 1518 as *"two cottages*

*J W Hayllar's original shop in at 87 High Street (1893)
and Mr H F Hayllar (1930s)*

called Mottes and Dies belonging to Hoddesdonbury Manor." The former was thatched and by 1728 had become the Red Lion Inn, while its next door neighbour also traded as an inn during the 17th century. These were superseded by this impressive new mansion in 1860.

A chemist's shop had originally been set up by Mr Coulson in 1835 further up the High Street in a very small, pokey store at number 87. This was purchased by Mr Green who later sold it on to James Hayllar – a Quaker - in 1893. By the end of the 19th century Mr Hayllar had re-located into a very smart shop here at the south end of the High Street and had bought his son Howard into the business, who subsequently took it over as sole proprietor in 1926 when his father died.

According to an advert in the *Journal* in 1935 celebrating the centenary of the business the busy Howard Frederick Hayllar was dispensing an astonishing 20,000 prescriptions each year from his one shop. *"While the business still retains the best of the old traditions, including its distinct 'family' nature, it is yet thoroughly up-to-date in its methods generally and stocks a very comprehensive range of those goods usually associated with a first class pharmacy. Evidence of the lengthy establishment of this highly reputable business is to be seen in a number of the original pharmacy fittings.'* In addition the chemist offered a photographic developing and printing service for your 'snaps'

In the late 1930s Mr Hayllar, married to wife Winifred and father of two daughters, was revealed in a *Journal* profile to be an extraordinarily busy and active member of his local community. *"A very keen sportsman and has been associated with many sporting associations of the district… he is an enthusiastic member of the Hoddesdon Swimming Club… and is now a*

Hayllar & Son's shop at 35, High Street (1933)

Vice President of the Hoddesdon Town Football Club and the Hoddesdon Cricket Club." In addition he was President of the 'Hoddesdon Tramps' hiking club, which he had helped to found; Secretary of the Congregational Church Guild; Vice Chair of the Hoddesdon & Rye Park Traders Association; a keen amateur photographer; local reporter for the *Hertfordshire Mercury* and 'Hoddesdon's Rainfall Recorder for the Air Ministry'.

Of course, this was before the advent of the National Health Service, as George Don reminds us. *"You used to pay four shillings a week for this health insurance system and then you could go to the doctors and then you went to Hayllars. Along the top shelf there were these great big glass jars full of this coloured liquid. Old Hayllar with his little glasses – I remember him. Behind him was all these drawers, wooden drawers where he kept all his stuff. It was all wood inside. He gave the impression he was not a man to be messed with – a strict man, but he would smile."*

Just after the war enlargements had to be made to the shop in 1947 which included a new waiting room for customers, owing to '*the very large increase in their dispensing work.*' Mr Hayllar also had a keen interest in local history and in 1948 he wrote *The Chronicles of Hoddesdon* which was published by Thomas Knight & Co. Ltd. Neville Townsend remembers another member of staff who had become crucial to the business by this time. *"Mr Hayllar was a licensed pharmacist, but he was getting old. His daughter - Mrs Edwards, a widow, I think - knew what there was to know, but she could only fulfil prescriptions when Mr Hayllar was around."*

Although he retired in 1967, the report of Mr Hayllar's death in the *Mercury* in 1969 showed that this well known local shopkeeper was still as busy as ever in his old age. *"Author, historian, meteorologist, chemist and collector extraordinaire, 79 year old Mr Howard Frederick Hayllar died at his home on Saturday evening... He was a member of several local organisations including the Hoddesdon Society, Hoddesdon Museum Committee and the East Herts Archaeological Society."*

By the 1980s the shop was occupied by the Grayt Expectations Kitchen Shop who subsequently migrated north to the former Staggs premises at the north end of the High Street.

FAMILY BUSINESSES

As we've now been introduced to several of the many family-run shops that served the residents of Hoddesdon for decades, it seems like a good time to stop for a moment or two and consider the ways in which those independent businesses and their owners formed the backbone of the local community for nearly a century.

From the 1880s onwards Hoddesdon was a prosperous town with a growing and increasingly affluent population. Edward Paddick paints a delightful picture of the town at turn of the 20th century when he was a boy: *"The High Street was lit by gas lamps and those who are used to the uniform lighting of the street today would probably be surprised at the gaiety of the night scene when, because of the poor light from the street lamps, nearly every shop had its own lamp or lamps above its shop window of varying design and size giving to the street, on a clear night, a fairy-like appearance."*

Of course Hoddesdon was very much a country town, much to the delight of Peter Shepherd growing up in the 1920s and 30s. *"Well, living in Paul's Lane, of course the fields were 200 yards or so from where we lived, just down across from the brook on the lane, and then you were in to the fields. The farm - Geddings Farm - was there; Jersey cows were in the fields, which is now Norris and Winterscroft Roads - they were all fields in my day; mushrooms you could collect in general. We had a perfect life for young boys. Play cricket and football in the fields. What more do you need at that age?"*

Olive Knight is of the same generation: *"We had a lovely toyshop called Cousins, and lots of other lovely shops too… ladies dress shops, two gents outfitters, three or four grocers, two fishmongers, bakers - so that you could have a lovely time just walking through Hoddesdon shopping."* Peter Shepherd adds: *"I remember the shops in Hoddesdon being mainly on the small side, but they were always very friendly, local people mainly served in them, to my memory."*

During 1930s the Hoddesdon & District Traders Association and Chamber of Commerce would organise an annual 'Shopping Event'. In 1936 prizes worth £60 were given away over the six day long promotion. There was a 'Mystery Man' who shoppers had to stop and challenge with a certain phrase – if successful they were given vouchers which could be used in local shops displaying a special 'yellow circle'. Shoppers voted for the best dressed shop window; there was a 'spectacular balloon release' in the market place – some balloons having valuable vouchers attached; and there was a painting competition for children. Over fifty High Street shops are listed as participating.

Of course, most people were forced to shop locally due to the fact that they couldn't afford their own transport, as Dorothy Chilton reminds us. *"There weren't any buses when I was small. The buses came down from London in the summertime to Wormley and they used to turn round and go back. Then a bit later on the 'people's buses', which were brown, ran from Nazeing through to Hertford via Stanstead. You could stop them anywhere – there were no stops, you just put your hand out. And then the national buses – they were the green ones – they only used to go along the Ware Road. They would go straight down to Waltham Cross and then we would get a tram to go into London."*

Home delivery was also the norm in the first half of the last century, long before the practice was revived in the internet shopping age, as Peter Shepherd recalls. *"Many things were delivered by horse and cart. The milk, for example, was horse and cart with milk churns and three ladles - half pint, pint and quart - so that you took a jug out and the milkman or milk lady would dip the corresponding ladle in and fill up the jug. The horse never needed to be told where to go; he just went on his own and stopped outside the house where he'd got to go."*

The practice continued well into the 1950s, as William Smith confirms: *"Well the bread was delivered by Parker's Bakeries. The man that drove the cart, it was a brown horse, with a canopy cart at the rear, and it had sort of hanging things at the back, for horse buckets and wheat and barley and oats for the horse to feed on… we used to run up and jump on the back of it because of the metal things, four kids hanging off the back of the cart."* Parrott Brothers, who had a yard in Amwell Street, were contracted to carry out the street cleaning for Hoddesdon UDC – as a boy Tim Turner remembers *"a one-legged road sweeper. We used to see him on the way to school at St Cross. He had a wooden crutch and used to hold the broom in one hand. He had a horse and cart."*

Even evacuees arriving during the early years of the war, like Joan Umney, were made welcome by the locals. *"It was just a very quaint town, nice friendly people and nice little shops, cafes, restaurants, the pubs, the old garage at the top of the High Street. My mum got to know a lot of people.* "According to George Don, the town centre in the 1940s was a much less congested place than today: *"Cars were not that plentiful at the end of the war and they used to park on the right hand side of the High Street. There were more people you would know when you walked along the High Street as people were more local then."*

The two decades before and after the Second World War can probably be characterised as the hey-day of the independent retailer which is what I want to celebrate in this book. These entrepreneurial and energetic men, and a few women too, were the pillars of the local community and often

Shop owners (1958) Back row left to right - Mr S F Norris, L Hitching, L W Sharp, R Smith, H C Stagg with the trumpet. Front row left to right – L Nuttall, W J Haward, R F C Ross, A Greenward.
Crouching centre – D W Reynolds.

involved in a breath-taking range of local organisations, sports clubs and charities. Many also served on the District or County Councils - all in addition to bringing up families and running a full time business! We see a group of the leading shop owners of that period in a photograph *(previous page)* which appeared in the *Journal* in December 1958.

Around the same time the paper also ran an article written by a new resident of the town entitled *'A Satisfied Customer'*. *"How does Hoddesdon strike a newcomer? Perhaps the first and most lasting impression is its air of cleanliness, the High Street light and airy, the shops clean and well kept. And how helpful and courteous the shopkeepers and assistants are – a refreshing change from so many of those in London... Hoddesdon has an air of prosperity; not the boom style but a quiet prosperity resting on a sure foundation and this is reflected in the way the trades people treat their customers."*

By the 1950s more people were able to afford their own cars, like Neville Townsend's family. *"As my mother was a teacher and did not drive, my father did quite a lot of the shopping as he had a car except for a brief period in 1952/3. So, although we lived in Broxbourne, quite a lot of shopping was done in Hoddesdon. My father always tried to go to those shops kept by British Legion members as he spent a lot of his leisure time helping the Legion."*

The south end of the High Street decorated for the Coronation of George VI with Home and Colonial and International Stores on the left (1937)

Peter Haynes fondly recalls his home town as a place that still had great charm and character. *"In the 1950s Hoddesdon was, what I supposed we regarded as, 'a lovely old town.' We still had the lovely High Path going up Amwell Street; we still had most of the buildings. Amwell Street was, of course, just a row of old cottages built in the 19th century, some of them the 18th century probably, and it was a busy road because it was the A10 and it went through to Ware...We had a lot of lovely buildings in the town which we lost, sadly."*

And so we now turn back to resume our tour.

CLABOURS (37, High Street) currently Shepherds Estate Agents

In the early 1900s this was the site of a Watchmaker & Jeweller's shop run by Charles Watson Dawson assisted by his two sons Ted and Bruce. In December 1935 A A Bond of Waltham Abbey purchased Dawson's business and after the Second World War moved up the High Street. In their place was an opticians run by A R Bond – possibly a member of the same family. In a 1939 advert they warned local residents of the need for their services. *"During long blackout evenings almost everybody is doing more close work, and we are generally doing such work in the lowest possible strength of light. Do not run the risk of impairing your sight by imposing unnecessary strain on your eyes."*

In March 1945 another change of ownership took place and the townsfolk of Hoddesdon who could afford it now had the chance to purchase expensive and fashionable furs from Clabours. Tim Turner describes the shop in the 1950s as *"very dark and dingy,"* but the business was still around in the early 1970s, also offering alterations according to Les Riches. *"My wife had a leather coat which she'd bought in London and the fashion changed and she had it shortened."* The politically incorrect furrier was gone by the 1980s, having been replaced by a branch of the Woolwich Building Society.

ARCHER & TURNERS (39, High Street) currently St Elizabeth's Charity Shop

Proudly advertising the fact that their business had been established way back in 1820 by Cornelius Prior, this up-market grocery store served local residents for over 150 years – in the early days being known as 'Turner, Archer & Turner'. Mary Newton's mother was a customer: *"you had lovely high stalls at the counter, and you were given pieces of cheese to try, and their wine cellar was downstairs, and they used to pop downstairs."* Dorothy Chilton knew the family who ran the shop which sold *"rather better class goods – they always smelt of coffee, ground coffee. Mr Dimmock worked there – his daughter was in my class. They sold all different sorts or teas and coffees and spices and that sort of thing."* Mary Young's family were not customers because *"to us it was an 'upper-class' shop, but I can remember the smell of the coffee being ground. And at the time we couldn't afford anything like that – for us it was Camp Coffee in a bottle. But later we were able to get the coffee beans from Meadows."*

Les Riches' best friend, Bill Lee, worked for the business as a delivery boy in the 1950s: *"he used to ride their trade bike with all the goods in. People used to come in from Broxbourne, and there were some quite wealthy people up in Broxbourne - I remember him telling me the 'Scholl' shoe people who made the sandals, they lived at Broxbourne. And he used to get the job delivering the groceries to them after school on the big old bike with the big basket on the front."*

DELLOW BAKERY (41, High Street) currently William Brown Estate Agent and National Westminster Bank.

In the early 1900s this old building housed a bakery owned and run by William Blomfield Dellow whose hobby was showing a string of trotting horses, for which he won many prizes. His son Stanley played the organ at the Congregational Church further up the street. It later became Page's Bakeries, with additional branches in Broxbourne and Ware. By the early 1960s it had been split into two retail units – on the south side was Elizabeth's Florists, with Arbon & Upton Estate Agents next door.

A few years later the property had been knocked down along with its next door neighbour (see below) and replaced with a bland two storey brick block with two retail units on the ground floor and offices above.

MITCHELL'S HODDESDON BAZAAR (43, High Street)

Mr Mitchell's stationers shop was also known as the 'Hoddesdon Bazaar' where the entrepreneurial owner sold his own series of postcards of the town produced just before World War I. In the 1930s Alan Cook's aunt, became the manager - one of only a handful of women running retail businesses in the town: *"they sold wool and all sorts of things... Her name was Mabel Cook."* It was another small shop that stocked a remarkably wide variety of different products which included, Paddick reveals, *"the canes by means of which the local school masters kept order in school."* Their 1939 advert offers: *'Diaries, Calendars, Greetings Cards, Gift Stationery.'*

Mable Mitchell (formerly Cook), Manager of Mitchell's 'Hoddesdon Bazaar' (1930s)

Mary Newton had to take shelter there during a wartime air raid. *"I was shopping in Hoddesdon with my mother, and I can remember the dog fights over the High Street. A particular one, we were all wondering what to do and the lady who owned Mitchell's bookshop then, she invited us all to come in and we all trooped down into her cellar under the shop."* By 1955 the business had been taken over by Wyman & Sons: Newsagents, Booksellers and Stationers where avid reader Les Riches was a regular customer. *"I still have my first 'Observer's Book of British Birds' in which, strangely enough, all the photos are black and white. Because this is 1948, or something like that."*

MIDLAND BANK (45, High Street) currently HSBC

Originally the site of a charming three storey brick building with a bow fronted entrance which was a private house in 19th century, around 1900 this had become a shoe shop run by Mr & Mrs Blackeby. The demands of modern commerce dictated that this property, which was occupied by Donald Hickling menswear until 1938, should be removed and replaced with another corporate edifice suitable for the Midland Bank which, several decades later, was absorbed into the global giant HSBC.

ACHILLE SERRE (47, High Street) currently Boots Opticians

This was a private home in the mid Victorian era, but around 1900 it had become the Hoddesdon Dairy kept by Ted Goodwin who grazed his cows

Achille Serre cleaners on the corner of Lord Street (1963)

in Admiral's Walk. It became known as 'Creameries' during World War I and was run by Miss B Willsmore and her sister for a Norfolk farmer, hence the sign for 'Holyfield Dairy Farm' which appeared above the entrance in the 1920s perhaps?

During the Second World War Miss Willsmore took over the enterprise with a partner and re-named it the 'White Heather Dairy', which then moved to Lord Street during the post war years. Achille Serre dry cleaners are operating from this site in 1963.

RUMBELOWS (49, High Street) currently Grafters Recruitment

Just before the First World War this building was the premises of Ashford's Estate Office, which had become Lewis & Hill Estate Agents and Auctioneers by the early 1920s. One of the staff was Mr R Siseman who started work there aged 16. In the 1930s most people rented property as very few could afford to buy their own – flats in the Hoddesdon cost from 10 shillings (50p) to rent, with a house starting at 14/6d (72.5p). By 1936 yet another draper and milliners shop named 'Daphne' was the new tenant.

From the 1950s this large corner premises on two floors was occupied by a branch of the Rumbelows chain which sold electrical goods, and their record department was one of Les Riches' favourite teenage haunts. *"That was run by a guy called Johnny Fry. He was also a good guitarist and used to play in one of the local groups... You used to go in the booths in Stones and listen to the records, the same over at Rumbelows where the record department was upstairs. We spent a lot of time in there before they moved down to Fawkon Walk on the corner – where New Look is now."* After Rumbelows departed, the building became a branch of the Bradford & Bingley Building Society in the 1980s.

BROCKET ROAD

This is where we turn left and take the first of our detours to visit a few places off the main drag. Until 1892 this was just a narrow track known as Oakden Lane after the farmer who owned the farm a little way down.

THE BOOK CENTRE (1B, Brocket Road) currently Flashdance

Eric Watson and his wife Caroline set up an independent bookshop 'The Book Centre' in 1967 in this bijou store, and ran it until June 1984 when they retired and sold the business to former publisher Peter Lardi.

The Book Centre just prior to the move to Fawkon Walk (1986)

Eric was reported in the *Mercury* as saying: *"We certainly enjoyed our time here and I'd like to think we made good friends with other shopkeepers and our customers. We haven't had a holiday for more than 17 years, so we're certainly going to have a bit of a rest."*

The new owner Peter Lardi told the paper, *"We want to provide a good service to people and the good books people want... There is room to browse around the Book Centre's well filled shelves and on them you will find much to thrill, educate and to wonder at, whatever your choice."* On their first day of business Peter remembers taking the grand sum of £135.

In October 1986 the Book Centre moved into larger premises at 26, Fawkon Walk, where son-in-law Toby Spencer joined Peter as joint proprietor, along with other members of their family who also helped in running the business. After Peter retired and handed over the business to Toby, the shop continued to thrive until the Sainsbury's store re-located to their enormous new site on the opposite side of the High Street.

The old precinct was left to deteriorate as shops closed down or moved out leaving the Book Centre as one of the last remaining retailers operating there. It finally closed in 2004 to make way for the demolition of the site for a major re-development programme *(see pages 46 and 116)*

Peter Lardi took over the Book Centre in 1984 and moved to Fawkon Walk in 1986 with son-in-law Toby Spencer as his new partner.

which included the construction of new flats, a branch of Aldi's supermarket, and a £2m health centre, which still remains empty in August 2014 - more than four years after it was completed.

KUCZA WATCH REPAIRS (3, Brocket Road) currently Flashdance

Just after World War II Polish émigré, Wlodek Kucza, learned the trade of a watch repairer on a British Government training programme and set himself up in this modest shop. In 1946 he married local girl Jean after a courtship that started while she was helping him learn English. Jean Kucza became a French teacher at Stanstead Road School in 1958, working there until her retirement in 1984. Having given up his business in 1967, Wlodek died in 1986, but Jean continued a very active life until her recent death in June 2014.

THE BROCKET ROAD STORES (18, Brocket Road) currently Sally B's Bar and Mexican Grill

On the left hand side further along we find this charming and very distinctive wooden building which was constructed in 1816 as Nazeing's first chapel. The whole edifice was moved to Hoddesdon in 1876 by builder William Hampton *(see page 14)* who originally re-erected it on stilts. Over the next 50 years it became a multi-purpose space to be rented out - as the HQ of the Hoddesdon Liberal Party, a regular venue for Salvation Army meetings, and it was also used as a gymnasium.

Edward Allen, Chairman of Hoddesdon Urban District Council, subsequently set up a cycle shop there and manufactured his own 'Brocket' bicycles on the premises. It later becomes the site of Lowfield Garage run by H C Arnold which opened from 7am to 8.30pm during the mid 1930s. Their adverts in the *Journal* offer *'Washing and polishing at keenest prices - High pressure greasing by Tecalemit Gun - Air, Regent Petrols and good variety of best oils.'*

By the 1950s the ground floor of this quirky building had been enclosed and become the home of Brocket Road Stores – a treasure trove of a place, consisting of an extraordinary mix of tools, DIY items, army surplus gear and architectural salvage. Les Riches has very fond childhood memories of the place his family nicknamed 'Junkies'. *"It was a gold mine. We've still got an ammunition box at home which came from there, all manner of stuff. Because it was constantly changing, even crockery and that sort of thing from the Cunard liners. It used to get crowded on a Saturday afternoon – all the stuff used to be out at the side of the alleyway and people used to browse along there and buy."*

Schoolboy Tim Turner was another regular weekend browser *"I think he bought stuff from the dockyards - naval surplus. We went here most Saturdays. Marvellous jumble of old stuff. I still use a string of coloured linen flags off a ship".*

A few years later a successful car designer called Ron Hickman rented the room above the stores and spent several years working on a new invention: a light, useful and cheap folding work bench. For several years he tried selling it to the major British tool manufacturers who all turned it down, until Black and Decker finally decided to offer it for sale as 'The Workmate' in 1973. It went on to sell over 30 million units in the next 40 years. Les Riches relates what subsequently happened. *"He went over to Brewery Road in the end... started a small engineering company in their old buildings – I suppose they were part of the old brewery. And it used to have 'Home of the Workmate' up on the sign. That was 1982."*

In the last decade this quirky property has been host to a bewildering number of different bars and eateries.

SHIRLEY'S WOOL SHOP currently Hoddesdon Town Dry Cleaning

Huddled in the shadow of its large neighbour, this tiny building served as the town's employment exchange from 1931-38, managed by Mr F T Attfield. By the 1960s it had become Shirley's wool shop; for the last decade it has been home to a succession of dry cleaners.

Brocket Road Stores and Shirley's Wool Shop (mid 1960s)

We now need to retrace our steps and return to the northern corner where Brocket Road meets the High Street.

BARCLAYS BANK (51, High Street) currently the same

Over 140 years ago this was where Hoddesdon's first bank opened in the 1870s - a branch of Tuke, Lucas & Seebohm in Hertford, built in 1847 by Christopher Tuck. John Warner's son Septimus was its first Manager, and in the early days the bank only opened on Tuesdays and Fridays from 10am to 1pm. The building was dismantled in 1892 to widen the entrance to Brocket Road, the cost being paid for by public subscription.

The property immediately next door on the north side was an inn around 1600, becoming a double fronted shop run by the Collings family who sold stationery and fancy goods during the Victorian period. It was taken over in 1896 by Sharples Bank which later changed to Barclay & Co. In the 1920s an institutionally-designed bank building replaced the old house, although Barclays felt the need to replace this yet again in 1975 with another unattractive, corporate lump of bricks.

THE CO-OP (53, High Street) currently Louise's Florist

George Bryant is the proprietor of a 'tobacconist and fancy stationer' in

Hoddesdon's first bank which was demolished in 1892 to widen the entrance to Brocket Road.

the late 1890s, but by 1918 his wife Ellen - another rare example of an entrepreneurial woman in that era - was selling tobacco both here and in a second outlet at 81 High St. By 1922 her son William is listed as proprietor of this latter shop.

The Enfield Highway Co-Operative Society had moved into these premises by 1963 – presumably awaiting the building of their new department store. *(see page 137)* Their original location was down in Amwell Street, where the organisation had opened the town's first Department Store in 1915. As Peter Shepherd recalls, it was *"about the largest shop in Hoddesdon. Inside the Co-op store were three departments: one was the grocers, and then I think the following one after that was drapers, and then outfitters, I think ladies fashion mainly. And at the back of that department was a dairy, so milk was delivered from there as well - so it was more a less a complete job in one."*

Joan Umney's mother was a loyal customer, *"because they used to have these 'mutuality cheques' and they were five shillings each and you used to get them in strips of about a pound. And you could use those to pay so much a week. You bought them from someone who came round to the house – a tallyman. So that's how we paid for our shoes – and I always remember saying to my mum 'Oh, we always have to have our shoes from the Co-op and they are always quite frumpy.' As a girl I hated that."*

George Don's family shopped there for the 'divvy' scheme. *"A lot of our stuff came from there because you used to get a dividend in those days – every year they'd pay a dividend. It was on a card."* The Co-op was still prospering well into the 1950s when William Smith's father was Manager of the store. However, the dated building was abandoned in the early 1960s and subsequently demolished in 1966 to make way for the building of the Dinant Link Road and Star roundabout. By the 1980s this has become an optician's practice run by Robert Hutchinson.

HEATHERS + BEEHIVE CAFÉ above (53A, High Street) currently Benvenuti

This very old building, probably dating from the 1550s, was still a private residence in the 1860s. By the interwar years it had been adapted for retail use. When alterations were made just after World War II traces of 17th century decorative stencilling were found on walls. Tregelles reminds us that *"changed as is the general appearance of Hoddesdon High Street, many of the brick fronts are but the casings of the ancient timber-built dwellings."* On the ground floor in the 1950s was Heather's newsagents, frequented by Joan Umney. *"We used to buy sweets in there – dolly mixtures, Fry's peppermint chocolate bar I used to have sometimes."*

A few years later on leaving school she was to get to know these premises exceptionally well, being employed by the Beehive Cafe up on the first floor run by the Cowley family. *"It was quite big – you went up the stairs and there was a massive kitchen and then three dining rooms... There was a big kitchen at the back where Janet and Ann were - they were the two daughters of the Cowleys. Janet was the cook and Ann used to help out, but she was more into office work. Mrs Cowley was a nice lady and she owned the place and worked very hard."*

The Cowley's living quarters were also in the two upper floors and Joan was allowed to use their sitting room for her tea break. Stairs from the back of the kitchen led down steeply to the rear of the property and Joan regularly had to negotiate these carrying large trays of rolls to be taken across to Danes' cleaning works off Brocket Road.

According to Joan the lunch menu was not fancy, but wholesome. *"It used to be sort of pies, sausages – basic, but nice food. I can't remember them ever doing chips – it was salads, meat and two veg, and I remember her doing 'toad in the hole'. And nice homemade puddings."*

Co-operative, Heather, the Beehive Restaurant and Easiephit (1963)

There was a tea shop serving home baked cakes made by Janet, with little silver tea pots and the jugs to match on a tray. Joan's uniform was a green check overall and green apron with mauve flowers. *"But you always had to look tidy obviously. You had to look after people and hope you'd get a tip because we didn't get paid a lot. And I did very well for tips. I think I used to get paid £1.10 shillings (£1.50) and I used to give my mum the £1.00 and have the 10 shillings left over for myself."*

Heather's were still in residence in the 1980s having had a glossy, contemporary makeover; they had switched to selling greetings cards, and moved their tobacconists and newsagents next door.

EASIEPHIT (55A, High Street) currently Panache Kids

By 1935 C A Bryant, a corn merchant and pet shop, sold budgerigars, canaries, foreign birds, goldfish and tortoises here. The retailer re-located to the opposite side of the street in the mid 1930s and by the early 1960s Easiephit, a discount shoe store, were based here. They were replaced in their turn by Garniers, the jewellers before they migrated north to Fawkon Walk. *(see page 116)*

Combat Stores and E W Nicholls (1963)

COMBAT STORES (57, High Street) currently Panache Baby

This property was the private residence of Mrs & Mrs Barnett and Mrs Albertus Hampton in 1870. Around the turn of the 20th century Dr J E B Wells ran a surgery there, but it had become Hoddesdon's first Employment Exchange in the 1920s. By 1963 this is the site of the rather trendy Combat Stores which also had branches in Ware and Bishops Stortford selling macho clothing for men; by 1968 they have been supplanted by a branch of Milletts.

E W NICHOLLS GREENGROCER (59, High Street) currently Bowmans

Another family run 'greengrocer and fruiterer' which had been trading in the town since the 1930s and survived through to the late 1960s. The same family name as the butcher further up the road.

ASHFORDS (61 – 63, High Street) currently Tesco Metro

Dating back to around 1570, this was the original site of Hoddesdon Post Office until it moved across the road to impressive purpose-built premises in 1893. The Post Master, Mr Ashford, apparently kept a rope with a hook on the end in his bedroom upstairs so that when the horse drawn post office van called at midnight and 3.30am he could haul up the sacks without having to go all the way downstairs and out into the cold.

James John Ashford re-located his grocery shop in Lord Street to this prime vacant spot on the High Street, and the north end of the same building became Mr Brooks' ironmongery store. By 1899 the business is being run by Charles Henry Ashford with additional stores in Rye Park and Wormley. He is followed in turn by William Ernest Ashford, who appears with his staff Mr Brown, Mr F Drane and Mr J Copping in a 1910 photo. By 1918 the building has been split into a confectionary shop called 'The Cabin' at 61 and a grocery store at 63. In 1935 'special value' offers in the shop included *'Empire Butter from 10d; finest cheese with flavour from 6d and finer qualities of choice tea from 1/4d.'*

Ashfords was bought up by F W Wash and Sons in 1949 – Brian Walsh, who worked for his family's business from his teenage years and subsequently became owner and manager of the shop, takes up the story. *"Our business first started in a small shop my grandfather bought which is near the Bull Pub in Broxbourne. The London side of that there's still a row of cottages – it was one of those. And they also had a drapers shop there and my grandmother ran the drapers next door. They had a bit of a struggle when they first started and actually they had a very good customer who lived opposite – Miss Thornton, if I remember rightly – and my grandfather did mention to her that they were in a bit of difficulty. And she offered to lend him some money to carry on with - on the condition that he attended church three times on a Sunday. Which he duly did apparently, and it got him out of that hole."*

Brian's father joined his grandfather in running the shop in the late 1930s, but was called up at the start of the Second World War where he served in the RAF for the duration. He came back into the Broxbourne business after being de-mobbed, but the family were keen to expand - hence the decision to buy Ashfords. *"The shops were all run on a traditional style counter service – a person behind a counter collecting goods for the customer in the shop,"* Brian remembers. *"I'm sure people have seen 'Open All Hours' – it was that type of thing. Of course, there was very little refrigeration in those days and when we bought in goods such as provisions – butter, cheese, bacon – they were all stored in a cellar underneath the shop. They were actually kept in very good condition because cellars have a good constant temperature throughout the year."*

In the 1950s the shop employed about 10 staff who had to become skilled in judging the weights and sizes of all these items. *"I was mainly weighing up loose products... in one of the rooms out the back weighing up sultanas maybe into pound bags, currants, all dried fruits – that was a big part of it. Weighing up sugar even. Virtually everything we bought was purchased in bulk and re-packaged on site, except for canned goods, of course."*

Like all their rivals the business ran a home delivery service, with three vans doing daily deliveries. The shop had no choice but to run a lot of credit and hope that people would pay up on time at the end of each month - which didn't always happen. *"A lot of it was people with very nice houses - country estates almost, sort of thing. I can remember one – I won't mention any names – where they used to welcome me in there when I opened the door: 'Come in, old boy. Sit down, do have a sherry.' Then he'd offer me a sherry and then he'd got this pile of papers on his desk and he'd be rummaging through them. 'I've got a cheque somewhere here for you. Well, I'll tell you what, I'll pop it in the post.' Then the same thing would happen the next time."*

Brian returned around the age of 22 to help his father full time and they quickly implemented a plan to expand the business. In 1951 they purchased the ironmongery next door from Mr Brooks and ran it as a separate shop until, as Brian remembers, *"we got fed up with counting out all the little screws and seeing coal buckets hanging off the ceiling...*

Meadows new self-service store (early 1960s)

So we pushed the shop back a lot further – we had a lot of room at the back fortunately, so we were able to go back. We bought a bakery the other side and we knocked that all into one large shop."

At the back of their old property, which had once adjoined the ancient George coaching inn, was a large barn originally used for stabling, with a hay loft above it which the shop now used for storage. However, as hygiene regulations became more stringent the Walsh's had it demolished in 1962 to build a modern brick storeroom in its place, which can still be seen today.

When self-service was introduced around 1960 the family decided the store needed a change of name and they chose to call it Meadows. For Brian and his customers this was all an exciting new shopping experience, with a whole new range of products. *"Birds desserts, Chivers or Roundtree's jellies that you dissolved. It was a huge change in the way we worked. Now there were new products appearing on the shelf every week... The prices before were your same prices every week and they were set by your supplier, which is fine, and we did make a good margin out of it. But then the pressure from the supermarkets – the Tescos of this world – came on and started reducing the prices."*

Demolition of the old barn at the rear of Meadows (1962)

In an attempt to cut overheads the company tried to bring in a delivery charge, but customers reacted negatively and so the service was scrapped. They became members of a local buying group with a small warehouse, which allowed the independent grocers to buy in bulk and get better deals with suppliers so they could compete on price. However, over time, minimum orders were constantly jacked up until the quantities were unrealistic to store even for their consortium.

"That was when we decided to specialise", admits Brian. *"We became more of a delicatessen – and we went for the more quality product. Tiptree jams were just one example – at that time the supermarkets just weren't interested – so it gave us a little bit of a breather, I suppose. And that worked for a while. We had to bring in special cold counters for delicatessen products. We tried to do our best – to get the detail of it right, if you like. Just make sure everything was spot on, best quality. "*

One of the shop's loyal customers was George Don's wife. *"Meadows – they were looked upon as a bit more up-market. Spices and stuff that you wouldn't find in other shops which my wife would go in to get there. And if you took in a bottle they filled it up with wine – there were these taps on small barrels and they fill your bottle with wine, sherry and things like that."*

*The Congregational Church with the original site of
the British Girls School to the left (mid 60s)*

The pedestrianisation of the town and the removal of free parking at the north end of the High Street *(see page 153)* hit their business badly, according to Brian, and so, *"we sold up about 20 years ago – about 94 or 95. We couldn't see a light at the end of the tunnel to be honest."* Ironically the new owners of Meadows later sold the building for a Tesco Metro and moved the deli a few doors up the High Street to their other shop which was re-named Heathers & Meadows. *(see page 53)* This business closed in 2012.

CONGREGATIONAL CHURCH currently Fawkon Walk

Following the English Civil War there were many different sects and religious groups who wanted a simpler form of worship outside of the established church, one of which was the 'Independents'. In Hoddesdon their original meeting place from 1780 was a house on the corner of Ware and Hertford Roads. In 1841 missionary William Ellis and his wife Sarah arrived at Rosehill in Lord Street, having met John Warner during a convalescent stay in the South of France. He befriended the couple and persuaded them that his home town was a delightful place to live. William became a pastor for the independent worshippers in 1847 and the congregation grew considerably. Money was raised by William and Sarah Ellis to buy the land in the High Street and a brand new Congregational Church was built and opened for public worship in April 1847.

The previous building had housed the George Inn – a very ancient property dating from around 1464. In the coaching era it had stabling for 40 horses. Paddick reveals a hidden secret of the site: *"It had for many years, brewed its own ale, and the source of water from which it was made, a 20ft well, remained intact beneath the church during its 120 years, and was filled in when the church was demolished in 1967."*

Mr and Mrs Ellis also helped form a Temperance Association. Mr Ellis was a keen botanist and brought back many plant specimens from his travels, especially orchids, and one particular rare variety with spurs on it about 12" long. Paddick writes: *"Mr Ellis's name became familiar with both amateur and professional horticulturalists in connection with the new plants introduced by him, particularly 'Angraecum sesqipedale', and he never failed to carry off prizes where he exhibited at flower shows at Crystal Palace and Regents Park."*

In 1888 Rev John C Evans was appointed Pastor and remained in his post for an astonishing 42 years until 1930. A British School for girls and infants was also set up in a small building next door to the church in 1846 with support from John Warner. By the late 1890s it had an average attendance of 212, overseen by Headmistress Miss Florence Adams. In the 1920s Mollie Muetzel was a pupil there. After the pupils were transferred to the new Haslewood School, the building became the church hall and was used as a meeting place for many local organisations, along with

Hare's grocery shop (1906)

Gibsons Greengrocers (1963)

jumble sales and other events. The church was demolished in 1967 to make way for the Fawkon Walk precinct.

GIBSONS GREENGROCERS (67, High Street) currently Fawkon Walk

The property that was here until the mid 1960s may have been over three centuries old; from the mid Victorian period it was a grocer's shop run by Mrs Hare – after her death around 1910 her assistant Mr Neave carried on the business. After they were bombed out in 1941 the Gibson family later moved their greengrocery store here. Young Les Riches had a particular reason to look forward to his visits back in the 1950s. *"It was one of those shops that didn't have a window as such – they had just a shutter that they used to pull down at night. Of course, people didn't have a lot of money and my mum, as a treat, on school holidays... we used to come back to Gibsons in the summer and they used to have fresh pineapples. And they used to cut them up in slices and you could buy a slice of pineapple for 6d and she used to buy me a slice."*

Gocher's Butcher's Shop (1963)

GOCHER'S BUTCHERS (69, High Street) currently Fawkon Walk

There was a house here as early as 1387, and by 1470 it was held by a knight named Sir John Stoner for an annual rent of 17d – it was not an inn at this time, but was known as 'The Fawkon (Falcon) on the Hope' (Hoop). By 1539, it appears as 'Le Fawkon upon the ryng' and belonged to Sir Thomas Thorowgood whose daughter married Sir Marmaduke Rawdon, and so the property passed into the ownership of that family.

Towards end of 17th century the building we see in the 1963 photo above had been built and became the Griffin Inn - named after the heraldic beast featured on the Rawdon coat of arms. However, it didn't last long as an inn and its name was later taken over by another inn nearby. From 1700 onwards it housed a butcher's shop which, by 1890 had been run for about 30 years by the Tuck family whose premises, according to Paddick, *"had two lovely bow-fronted windows and a canopy ran the length of the building supported by wooden pillars at the edge of the pathway, as was common to butcher's shops in the 18th and early 19th centuries."*

By the turn of the twentieth century the business was owned and run by Mr Turner who was succeeded around 1925 by the Gocher family. In 1935 they were offering: *'Home Killed Prime Scotch Beef and Mutton. Pork Sausages a Speciality.'* In the 1950s Annette Marples was sent there by her mother to pick up the family's meat order. *"That's where my mum used to go. But Mrs Mills, who used to take the money - my sister and I were absolutely petrified of her, because she used to sort of give you a look as if to say, 'What are you doing in here?'"* Joan Umney collected meat for the Beehive Restaurant. *"You went up steps and then they had the big wooden counters which they just scrubbed every day. They were always nice there: 'Hello, dear, how are you?'"*

Brian Walsh at Meadows next door saw his neighbour regularly. *"Mr Gocher – I didn't know him that well, but he was certainly a formidable character in almost every way – probably a 'larger than life' character... He used to try to buy our place, actually. Because every time he used to go by the window and saw my father or myself in there he'd stop and then he'd mime counting out a wad of money and then walk off."*

Mr Gocher was a pretty entrepreneurial individual and operated a number of different strands to his business, as Brian Walsh explains: *"He had a slaughterhouse out the back – we used to sometimes hear the animals being slaughtered. Didn't take much notice in those days – probably would today. And, of course, he had the nursery behind there as well – the greenhouses."* In addition the *Journal* revealed in the 1950s that the butcher had even diversified into curing his own tobacco!

Mr Gocher in his tobacco curing shed (1950s) and Journal Advert (1938)

Architect's impression from the Hoddesdon Journal (1965)

Clearly a man to spot the opportunity for a great commercial deal it was Mr Gocher who sold his property and land to developers who subsequently built Hoddesdon's second shopping precinct in the mid 1960s – Fawkon Walk. The *Journal* reported that the first phase of building on the north side included a 7,500 sq ft Sainsbury's supermarket, 15 shops with offices above and the main unit fronting the High Street was to be a two storey department store for Pearsons of Enfield. There would be ample car parking for 160 vehicles that would access the new site via Brocket Road.

Completed in 1968, the precinct proved far more popular and successful than the larger Tower Centre *(see page 90)* and accommodated a mix of independent local shops alongside national chain stores. It underwent further development after Sainsbury's re-located to a large store which opened on the east side of the High Street in 2001. The whole west end of the site on the north side was demolished in 2007 to make way for a new Aldi store with an adjacent car park, retail units with flats above them and a new £2m Health Centre for the Amwell Street practice. *(see page 116)*

Unfortunately the recession hit at just this time, and the Beadie Group who owned the site went bankrupt in August 2009 just before the project was completed, leaving the medical centre unfinished. After several years of stalemate with the company's administrators, Broxbourne Council stepped in and bought the precinct in 2011 for £4.6m. However, despite repeated dates being announced for the opening of the medical facility, it still remained empty in August 2014.

Site demolition in progress for the Fawkon Walk development (1967)

PEACOCK'S BARBERS (71, High Street) currently Fawkon Walk

A barber called H Teddar was already working in this deceptively small property by the turn of the 20th century – in a period photo it advertised its services with a large red and white striped pole attached at right angles to

Fawkon Walk under construction (1967)

An advert from the Hoddesdon Journal (mid 1930s)
Mr F G Peacock and his daughter Gillian Rogers (1967)

the building. By the 1930s the business was being run by Mr Peacock, who had started working for the previous owner Mr E Belton at the age of 14. Just five years later at the age of 19 he was running the barbers shop himself. At this time the price of haircuts for men was sixpence (2.5p) and boys were charged four pence.

But, as Dorothy Chilton who worked in the same building explains, he was not the only occupant. *"There was the passageway that went through to Mr Peacock's saloon and then you went upstairs and there was a ladies hairdresser and the front room downstairs was a dressmaker's... Mr Peacock was rather slightly built and he had an apprentice."*

The photo of Dorothy *(page 49)* was taken outside her workplace about 1935 when she was 15. *"I was apprenticed to the dressmaker. I was there for about two years – because it was Miss Burrell who ran this dressmakers and she got married and her mother had a factory up in Ponders End making these commercial clothes so it faded out then."*

By 1955 Langham & Scott, Service Engineers were based downstairs and advertising a repair service for *'all types of radio receivers and domestic electrical apparatus.'* In 1967, after 44 years working in the barber's shop, Mr Peacock was leaving to make way for the new Fawkon Walk development. His married daughter Mrs Gillian Rogers who ran her hairdressing salon upstairs was losing her premises and was also uncertain about the future of her livelihood.

Dorothy Chilton standing outside 71, High Street (late 1930s)

SEATON'S NEWSAGENT AND CONFECTIONER (73, High Street) currently Fawkon Walk

Not surprisingly, this one was of Mary Newton's favourite childhood haunts. *"There was a tiny little shop - they used to also do the things for the Carisbrook Laundry, take in the laundry for them - but it was a little sweet shop. It couldn't have been more than the width of a door and a very small window, and it was lovely because she used to put all her sweets on little doilies on glass plates in the window, and if you wanted anything she used to have to lift up the flap and come in to the front and get it."*

FRANK ANDREWS SADLER (75, High Street) currently Fawkon Walk

Mssrs Long & Blundell were based here in the early 19th century; then William Carter established his shoe business in the premises around 1860 before re-locating to number 79 in 1865. *(see page 50)* Mr Billing was providing saddles and other specialist goods to the equestrian fraternity around the turn of the 20th century. Frank Andrews moved in to continue the same occupation, as well as running a Harness Maker & Cycle Shop in Stanstead Abbotts through the 1930s.

COUSINS GIFT SHOP (77, High Street) currently Clinton Cards

For centuries we'd have found the old Griffin Inn here – and in the late

1890s landlord Frederick Chapman ran a cab company from his premises. His successor in the Edwardian era was Mr Benham, who was also a jobmaster employing several coachmen. By the 1950s this was the home of Cousin's toy shop which moved from its original location on the opposite side of the High Street during the war.

CARTER'S SHOE SHOP (79, High Street) currently Books @ Hoddesdon

William Carter, son of a Buckinghamshire farmer, came to Hoddesdon with his young family in the early 1860s to set up a shoe making enterprise at 75 High Street. They moved two doors up in 1865 to 79. In the 1881 census William, described as a 'Boot & Shoe Manufacturer', and his wife Eliza are living with their two children: son and heir Charles, and daughter Sarah who later became a school teacher but never married. Three apprentices aged 14, 17 and 18 also lived on the premises with their employer. The business was obviously prosperous as we can tell from a set of portraits of the family taken in the 1870s.

Charles had a son, also named William, born in 1896 and two daughters Winifred and Doris. At the turn of the 20th century the Carters were promoting the shop as offering: *'a large & well assorted stock of boots and shoes to select from; repairs punctually and neatly executed.'* Up until 1913 all shoes were made to measure on the premises. A pair of ladies leather shoes cost 13 shillings and 6 pence in 1910 (67p in today's money). Shoe repairs were also carried out – soling and heeling a pair of men's shoes in 1910 cost 4 shillings and six pence (22p).

During the 1914-18 war William Carter joined the Queens West Surrey Regiment, seeing service in Mesopotamia and India. His grandfather William Carter died in 1925 at the age of 90, and Charles then took over ownership of the shop until his retirement in 1937. Although William had been an active member of both the Hoddesdon Cricket and Football clubs he began suffering from serious ill health, and his sister Winifred took over the running of the shop in the late 1930s and during the Second World War.

William's son Roy became the next generation of the family to operate the business when he was de-mobbed in 1944. He later married Marie and subsequently they bought up three sons in the family home above the shop premises. After what the *Hoddesdon Journal* described as *'a very long illness patiently and cheerfully borne'* William Carter died at the age of 60 in 1956. His funeral at the Congregational Church was well attended, with mourners including two of the shop's staff: Mrs Johnson and Miss Campkin.

Above:
William and Eliza Carter.
Right: *Charles and Sarah Carter.*
Below: *William John Carter (left) and Roy Carter (right) on right of photo.*

By this time the consumer boom of the 1950s had seen an explosion in new styles and trends in footwear. However, some things hadn't changed at Carters – *'jovial, bearded, 75 year old John Parker'* was interviewed by the *Hoddesdon Journal* in 1957 as he celebrated 45 years making, and later repairing shoes for the Carter family. When he started in 1912 he worked a 12 hour day and earned 30 shillings (£1.50) a week. Three years later Mr Parker finally retired, dying in 1962.

Dorothy Chilton was a customer. *"We got our better shoes there, and if we wanted our Wellington boots we went into Staggs on the other side of the High Street. They sat you down at Carters and bought you the shoes and tried them on. The men's department was at the front, the ladies further back."* Mary Young was taken there as a child. *"My mother bought my shoes in Carters – it was very good because I can remember them measuring my feet – which they don't do nowadays, which they should. When you came in downstairs through the front door there was a row of seats – and Mr Carter used to come and measure your feet."*

In 1967 the current owner, Roy Carter, was planning to celebrate the centenary of his family's business with a major re-vamp of the shop. The modernisation, which he told the *Journal* would provide *'a new heart for an old body'*, included an expensive new shop front and a smart carpeted interior of double the previous size with separate sections for men, women and children.

Roy Carter died in 1969 and his widow Marie carried on the business until she re-married and decided to sell the premises in 1973, when the shop

Advert from Hoddesdon Journal; Veteran employee John Parker (1957)

finally closed, having been run by the same family for an astonishing 108 years. Shortly afterwards the new shop front was subsequently ripped out to be replaced by the mock Victorian façade it still has today, and the Shoe Box opened to sell ladies shoes for the next thirty years.

BRYANTS TOBACCONIST (81, High Street) currently Keech Hospice Charity Shop

The Bryant family opened this second shop by 1918, with both shops initially being run by Ellen Bryant – although by 1922 she is running just this branch at the age of 67. A 1936 advert states '*We have a fine selection of Cigarettes, Tobacco, Cigars (British and Havana), Pipes, Pouches, Lighters (of many descriptions), Cigarette Cases, Wallets.* Hedley Eariss bought his sweets here in the 1950s."*It also specialised, that one, in tobacco. And it had quite a reputation for that. People would come from a long way around to get specialist tobaccos from that one."* It was later the location of Heathers & Meadows combining an eclectic combination of greetings cards, art and craft materials, a cafe and a delicatessen.

HICKLINGS MENSWEAR (83, High Street) currently Oxfam

In the early part of the last century Mr Eason ran his drapery store here; by the early 1960s it housed a ladies boutique run by Arthur William House, and Donald Hickling Menswear was still selling clothes here from 1938 through to the 1980s - but to the opposite sex.

SYLVIA BRYANT – WOOLSHOP (85A, High Street) currently Card Factory

In 1936 Central Radio Stores moved from round the corner in Lord Street, announcing their re-location with an enticing competition: '*Win a Free Trip for Two to America in the Queen Mary or across Europe by Air Liner or to any station on a Mullard Dial. Arrange your set of 'shuffle pictures' in correct order to win!*' By 1939 Woodside P F Products have taken over the premises to sell '*Eggs and Chickens, Golden Meadow Butter & St Ivel Dairy Produce, Milk.*' They also advertise '*Fresh Trapped Rabbits ordered by Monday for delivery Thursday.*'

Sylvia Bryant had opened a wool shop here by the early 1950s. In January 1955 she reminded her customers: '*WINTER has arrived at last – Never mind, equip yourselves with FUR GLOVES and SCARVES and look forward to a choice selection of Spring Millinery.*'

According to Evelyn Dellow, who was a friend of the owner, Sylvia ran her store with her mother who looked after the millinery department upstairs. It had lots of small inter-connecting rooms and went a long way back, as did many of the shops along that stretch of the street. She was a member of the Meek family who ran the gift shop down at the south end of the High Road. Her husband George was in the Guards armoured division in World War II and worked for Haward's builders subsequently. The couple were friends with the owners of Cousins toyshop and staunch members of Conservative Club.

Sylvia continued to live in the flat above her shop after she retired and sold on the business which was re-named Countryside Wools. On the night of August 9th 1996 a deliberate fire was started downstairs and the elderly Sylvia had to be rescued from her home which was badly damaged. Fortunately she was offered temporary accommodation in a flat opposite on the corner of Conduit Lane.

J W NICHOLLS UNDERTAKERS AND BUILDERS (85, High Street) currently Card Factory

This building was originally part of the Thorowgood estate and served as an inn at some time earlier in its existence. In the late Victorian period Mr J W Williams' builders firm superseded the one that Mr Nicholls had started here in the 1880s, and the Phoenix Fire Office operated from the top floor. When veteran resident Mollie Muetzel (originally Brewster) was born here in 1925 the business retained the original owner's name but was instead run by her father. She still has vivid memories of her childhood

Eason's Drapery and J W Nicholls Undertakers & Builders (1897)

home. *"When I lived on the High Street there, it was a little old fashioned market town, and it was beautiful. My earliest memories are leaning out of the window and seeing all the cows and sheep in the market right opposite my house. Father had the undertakers, builders, and plumbers business in the High Street, and my grandparents ran the Bull Hotel... We had a lovely sawmill - we used to make all our own coffins."*

Mollie lived there for the next 22 years until she left home to get married, but her father was forced to sell up in the early 1950s due to ill health. The business was bought by one of Hoddesdon's richest and most successful entrepreneurs, Mr Haward, to become part of his diverse local business conglomerate. *(see page 143)* In his teenage years Hedley Eariss became an occasional employee. *"I went to school with the undertaker's son. And at weekends and evenings as we got older, rather than his dad calling out other members of staff, sounds a bit morbid - but if a body had to be collected we would go with him with a coffin to bring the bodies back to the mortuary."*

By the 1970s the undertakers had changed hands again and were owned by Powell of Ware. I was told a story by someone who went there to enquire about funeral arrangements and found an empty office with just a

Donald Hickling and Nicholls Funeral Parlour (1963)

telephone on the desk and a notice for visitors to phone a certain number. The person made the call and was asked to make themselves comfortable and someone would be available to deal with them shortly. They waited patiently for an assistant, who eventually appeared a bit out of breath having jumped in a car and driven hot-foot from Ware!

PEARCE'S BAKERY (87, High Street) currently Café Nero

This was the site of one of the town's oldest inns – the Chequers or 'Les Chekkers' - with a large orchard to the rear which lasted until some time in the 17th century when it became a private house. This building has been used as a bakery for nearly a century – originally run by James Roberts, it was later taken over by Pearce's of Hertford who ran it as a branch of their local chain of shops until the firm suddenly collapsed in 2005.

THE BULL HOTEL (89, High Street) currently Peacocks

This iconic edifice, which dominated Hoddesdon's High Street for some 400 years, was originally known as the Bell Inn as far back as 1575 when it was rented by Thomas Fuller from Hoddesdonbury Manor. Tregelles informs us: *"In 1578 John Squyer is noted as 'keeper of the lodging house called the Bell,' and John Sommers, bailiff to Lord Burghley, complains that although the plague is in the house Squyer refuses to close it, and still receives passengers coming to the court."* It had probably been re-named the Bull by the early 17th century. There was another inn next door to the north called the Dolphin way back in 1378, but by 1596 this seems to have been amalgamated with its neighbour.

The hostelry had become nationally renowned after featuring in *Down Hall* - a popular 18th century epic poem written in 1715 by Matthew Prior.

Come here, my sweet landlady, pray, how d'ye do?
Where is Cicily so cleanly, and Prudence, and Sue?
And where is the widow that dwelt here below?
And the ostler that sung about eight years ago?
And where is your sister, so mild and so dear
Whose voice to her maids like a trumpet was clear?

By my troth, she replies, you grow younger I think;
And pray, Sir, what wine does the gentleman drink?
Why now let me die, Sir, or live upon trust,
If I know to which question to answer you first:
Why things since I saw you most strangely have varied,
The ostler is hang'd, and the widow is married.

And Prue left a child for the parish to nurse,
And Cicily went off with a gentleman's purse;
And as to my sister, so mild and so dear,
She has lain in the churchyard full many a year.

The Rev William Jones, curate and vicar of Broxbourne Church, whose diary was published in the 19th century, wrote about a memorable evening at the hostelry in February 1806. *"Yesterday the body of old Mr Milward was buried and the doctor and myself sat down with the executors and a large party at the Bull Inn, Hoddesdon. Much wine was drunk at and after a plentiful and elegant dinner. Twice or thrice only in my professional life have I joined such a set of merry mourners. I felt most uncomfortable afterwards."* The grand pillars at its front door were added in the early 19th century. During this period the landlord was Samuel Girling, who was succeeded in 1858 by Frederick Waters.

In 1812 the Hotel hosted meetings of the town's first sickness benefit group called the Union Society, which held an annual feast in July. They allowed a maximum membership of 41 people who had to abide by strict rules. *'If any member curse or swear at meetings he shall forfeit three pence for each offence... If any member shall come into the club room disguised in liquor he shall forfeit six pence.'* The Hotel became the headquarters of the town's first Friendly Society: the Odd Fellows in 1847, which later held an annual march through the High Street.

The Bull Hotel (c1900)

It had its sign hanging on a wooden beam directly over the main road through the town from 1620 onwards, as did the nearby Swan and Salisbury. Tregelles tells us: *"there is a tradition, probably of fact, that a man who had been a soldier once threw a cricket ball over all three beams. To clear the three he must have thrown at least 130 yards."* According to local legend a ghost was said to perform late night acrobatics on the beam.

The outer end of the beam from the Bull was supported by the town's Market House which had been constructed in 1634. The town's most eminent citizen, Sir Marmaduke Rawdon,*"besides his advice and assistance therein gave fortie pounds towards the finishing of it."* Timber was supplied by Lord of the Manor William Cecil, Second Earl of Salisbury, the rest of the funding came from other wealthy residents.

Initially called the 'New Town House' it was built of oak covered in carving, measured 50ft x 40ft and had a stairway in the north-east corner leading to an upper room which was later used for public meetings and entertainments. Tregelles says: *"Its north end was used as a stall, sometimes by a butcher, at other times by travelling hawkers. Posts were set in the narrow way between it and the adjoining houses to prevent cattle from passing. Its last use for a public purpose was at the time of the county election following the Reform Bill of 1832."*

By this time the Thursday market had declined to the point that the people of Hoddesdon petitioned the Earl of Salisbury to have their dilapidated old Market House demolished as they claimed it made the road narrow and dangerous. It was removed in 1833 and the carvings taken to Hatfield House where they were used to adorn the chapel. The over-arching sign from the Bull was removed in 1834. According to the 1891 census, the Bull was managed by William Miles and his wife Barbara; his mother lived there too along with their six children.

Mollie Muetzel (nee Brewster) also remembers the Bull Hotel with great affection as her grandparents were landlords – the Griffins took over in 1908 and stayed for the next 20 years. *"It was a carriage place originally... My grandmother used to collect sovereigns throughout the year and would give her husband a handful of sovereigns for Christmas. But I'm sure she used to hide them all over the hotel. So when they pulled it down, I'm sure they must have found some sovereigns here and there, in*

Wedding Party at the Bull in 1917 featuring Mollie Muetzel's family.

the alcoves and behind brickwork and things." Her uncle had a small hut in the old coaching yard where he ran one of the town's first taxi firms.

A wonderful photo from Mollie's family album shows the wedding party for her parents at the Bull on 21st September 1917. At the age of 83 and 81 respectively the Griffins featured in the *Hoddesdon Journal* in 1941 celebrating their diamond wedding anniversary. *(page 60)*

By 1935 Mr T Morris was proprietor offering '*Lunches, Dinner and Teas plus a large front saloon with a full sized billiard table which can be hired by the hour'*. William Smith attended a wedding there in the 1950s. *"They had a nice tea garden at the back. My aunt, she married an air force man from outer Cambridge, she was married at the St Paul's Church and she had the wedding reception at the Bull pub. They had a beautiful garden in the back there, and we spent the whole afternoon there drinking and eating."*

Hedley Eariss was less enthusiastic about the old building. *"In the mid sixties, I learned to drive, and the Bull was still there. We lived in Lord Street and the Bull had a canopy coming over the pavement, with two big round pillars that held it up. When you were trying to pull out of Lord Street, those pillars were right in your line of sight and it was terrible coming out of there."*

Mollie's grandparents Mr & Mrs Griffin (1941)

In 1961 news leaked out that plans were being put forward to build new shops in the High Street which involved the demolition of the grand old Bull Hotel. Many local residents were appalled at the prospect, and an inaugural meeting to set up the 'Hoddesdon Society' took place at Esdaile Hall on 15th September 1961. Mr E Bartleet became the first Chairman, and Committee members included Hoddesdon Urban District Councillor, L F R Jones, who was an architectural journalist. Former town librarian and local historian, Edward Paddick, gave a talk on the long and interesting history of the threatened hostelry.

Like today, planning applications had to be approved by local councils, but at that time there was very little concern about public consultation or considerations of how new building projects might impact on the infrastructure and general environments of towns and the lives of local communities. All modern building development was promoted as "progress" which, by definition, had to be a good thing.

The fight by the Hoddesdon Society and other concerned residents to save the Bull began in earnest when Hoddesdon UDC turned down the application to demolish the building on the grounds that it was on the Ministry of Housing and Local Government's statutory list of buildings of historic of architectural interest. A Public Enquiry was therefore announced. '*Can the Bull be Saved – Do the Public Care?*' asked the headline in the *Hoddesdon Journal*.

The debate went national when two members of the Hoddesdon Society appeared on the BBC Home Service programme *'Town and Country'* in April 1961. Mr Edward Paddick told the reporter: *"Take away the Bull Inn and the whole character of the main street will be altered. Hoddesdon just won't be Hoddesdon any more. Historically this building is worth saving. It is a hotch-potch of styles, but that only makes it more interesting."* Miss Sheldon of Lord Street told the programme she feared the town would become *"ugly... like Harlow."*

At a Public Enquiry on 3rd October 1961 the majority of speakers and residents were firmly against the loss of their most iconic building. Mr Paddick spoke for most people when he said: *"Let those who have it in their power to act, see that we have a town of picturesque usefulness and not one resembling a suburban planner's dream of dismal utilitarian uniformity."* However, the Government's Planning Inspector disagreed and the Minister subsequently backed his view that *"a suitably designed new building could replace the Bull without detriment to the street scene."*

The demolition of the Bull was completed in 1964. In its place Hoddesdon got its first purpose-built supermarket – a hideous, utilitarian slab that initially housed a Gateways store. Peter Shepherd felt the same way as

Demolition of the Bull Hotel (1964)

many locals. *"I remember the demolition of the old Bull Hotel, with sadness really because, in my opinion, it was a feature certainly that should have been left. As the replacement is quite a hideous thing in comparison - but I suppose that's what they call 'progress'."*

The floodgates now opened for developers and, despite the Hoddesdon Society's best efforts, the northern half of the town was bull-dozed to make way for The Tower Centre. *(see page 90)* It was not until the late 1960s that the Society was able to score its first substantial victory in helping to stop the destruction of Rawdon House. *(see page 169)*

BRADLEYS (91, High Street) currently empty

In the 1840s this large corner site at the junction with Lord Street was the printing works of a Mr G Dickinson who advertised himself as a *'Printing Office and Fancy Depository... Archery, Fishing Tackle, Stationery, Printer & all kinds of Fancy Goods at reduced prices.'*

1853 saw the formation of the Hoddesdon Mutual Improvement Society and for the second half of 19th century it rented the first floor of this building as a reading room, recreation area and a library where members

Bradleys Menswear (1963)

met, talked, and had access to books, magazines, etc. On the ground floor Church & Son are running a *'Gent's Hosiers and Outfitters'* for the next five decades from the turn of the 20th century. By the 1960s they have been replaced by Bradleys Gentlemen's Outfitters, and the town's exclusive stockist for Jaeger.

LORD STREET

Once again we are going to turn to our left and make a slightly longer diversion up Lord Street – formerly known as 'Lord's Lane'.

THE FRIENDS MEETING HOUSE

This austere building was opened for worship by local Quakers in 1829 and was used by many distinguished local Quaker families throughout the 19th century, including the Warners and the Borhams whose graves can now be seen at the rear of the property underneath a massive old elm tree. Elderly Metford Warner remembered accompanying his grandparents John and Sarah who were driven there in their Brougham for the service on 'first days' (i.e. Sundays). *"I had, on at least one occasion, sat on that most uncomfortable of all little hard seats facing my grandparents, he in Quaker coat & hat with the drab gaiters which sister Alice had assisted to button, & grandmother in her Quaker bonnet and becoming shawl."*

A predictably plain hall and meeting room were built adjoining the chapel in the 1920s which were used by numerous local groups until the beginning of the 21st century. In 2011 the members of the local Society of Friends had shrunk to so few that they decided to stop using the building for services - it is currently empty and its future uncertain.

HODDESDON POLICE STATION

A new purpose-built Police Station was constructed here in 1883 – up until that time the local constables had been located in a room at the base of the Clock Tower. *(see page 102)* In the late 1890s Robert Welling is listed as the Police Inspector in charge.

ROSEHILL

There was a lovely residence further up on the north side known as Rosehill built in the late 18th century when, Tregelles tells us, *"it was inhabited by the Misses Kemp, four maiden ladies who took much interest in their poorer neighbours of Lords Lane; but the name is a reminder of several of the old houses in Hoddesdon called 'The Rose'."* Rosehill was later owned by John Warner who rented it out to Mr and Mrs Ellis as their home for many years. During World War I it became a VAD hospital, then in 1926 Joseph Gurney Barclay moved in with his family. The property was sold off and knocked down in 1955.

HIGH LEIGH

This site first appears in a deed of 1403 with the name 'High Wyches'. Paddick suggests: *"It is mentioned again under the same name in 1535, but no occupier is named; it was probably nothing more than a group of farm buildings used only by the tenants of the Common Fields."* According to Tregelles: *"In 1677 it had become 'High Grounds' and was held by a John Holder, but I can find no mention of a mansion there... though it is said that there was then an old farmhouse on the spot."*

Charles Webb, a manufacturer of gold lace who made his fortune during the Crimean War, built a grand mansion for himself on the site in 1851 with lovely gardens laid out by Paxton. The following year he was allowed to divert the course of Lord Street further to the north so he could have greater privacy and build an impressive drive up to the house.

The property was subsequently purchased by Robert Barclay of the banking dynasty in 1871 and re-named High Leigh. Robert was born in Leyton in 1843. He served as Head of the branch of Barclays of Ury, Scotland, then moved on to become a partner in Messrs Barclay, Bevan, Tritton & Co, and had become a Director when the firm became a Limited Liability Company. He married Elizabeth Foxwell Buxton in 1868.

He enlarged the house, as well as improving and extending the grounds, which included the building of a new entrance lodge accessed via a stone bridge close to Cock Lane. Tregelles tells us: *"In the autumn of 1880 the avenue of Beech Trees between Rosehill and Lowfield was planted by Mr Barclay... and the cricket and football ground laid out for the public benefit, though still part of High Leigh."* He also gave the land adjacent to Beech Walk for the building of 'cottages for the aged poor' in 1897 to mark the Diamond Jubilee of Queen Victoria.

Mr Barclay served as JP for county of Hertfordshire, Chairman of the Cheshunt Bench and in 1893 was made High Sheriff of Hertfordshire. He was a Churchwarden of Hoddesdon Parish Church and financed the building of St Cuthbert's Church in Rye Park. After his death in July 1921 at 77 the house was sold to become a Christian Conference Centre which it remains today. The Barclay family decided to give parts of the grounds of High Leigh to the town by 'Deed of Gift' in June 1935 to become a park for the townspeople.

High Leigh from the garden (1950s)

Mollie remembers that day well. *"When they opened Barclay Park to the public - and I was there at the gates at the opening - I wasn't really very happy, because until then we'd reckoned that all of Barclay Park was more or less our personal playground. And in the woods - we knew every stick in the little woods there, which was really good."*

We now turn left at the bottom of Beech Walk, which lost many of its original trees in the 1960s, turn left again along Rosevale and then turn right back into Lord Street and return to the High Street where we left it.

LORD STREET COFFEE TAVERN (93, High Street) currently Swagga

The north corner of the Lord Street junction was originally the site of an ancient farmhouse known as 'Grace's' dating back to the owner Robert Grace in 1321. Next door was a three storey house, probably of 17th century origins, with a store on the ground floor selling china, stoneware and household utensils. The old Hertford Road originally began here leaving a green just to the north running up to the chapel.

A new Coffee Tavern was built in 1882 on land given by Robert Barclay to the Warner family to encourage temperance by offering non alcoholic drinks such as lemonade and hop ale from 6am until late evening. Tokens worth 2d were given away to redeem at the 'Three Cups Tavern'. Hayllar explains: *"This in its time served a very useful purpose in providing cheap meals somewhat on the lines of the transport cafes of today."*

In the late 1890s the Tavern's meeting room was being used as the venue for the meetings of the Hoddesdon Urban District Council on the last Wednesday of each month at 6.30pm. At this time it consisted of 12 members including Charles Christie, ironmonger Thomas Gardiner, Teddy Lock from the Drapers, with John A Hunt, the builder, as Chairman; Howard L Warner was Vice Chair and his father Septimus served as Hon Treasurer.

By the 1930s the building had been split into two shops. Drury Bothers were selling menswear in the larger site at number 93A. Their 1947 advert promises ration-weary customers: *'All the Year Round We Offer BEST VALUE for Your Clothing Coupons.'* Another tiny retail unit appeared on the side of the building in Lord Street and in the early 60s E M Gust ran a Jewellery business there, which later became the new home of another Jeweller: D W Reynolds.

WARD'S NEWSAGENTS (93B, High Street)

After Mr Dorrington closed his barber's shop, this small unit became the second newsagent and tobacconist shop run by the feisty Miss Tina Ward. Christened Lillian Mary in 1910, she was so small her family nickname was 'tiny' which became 'Tina' - the name she is still known by today at the remarkable age of 104. Tina explains: *"When I left school at 14 I had to come up to Hoddesdon to help my father who ran the newsagents when my mother became very ill. My mother died, which broke my heart. Although my father was a good man, he was so strict it made me a little bit afraid of him."*

The shop was a newsagent called E Ward - the E being for Edward, her father's name - and it sold tobacco, sweets and stationery with the family living in a flat above, as was usual at the time. When Tina's father died she took over running the store because her brother, who was an artist, didn't want to be involved. But Tina had a real problem. *"I wasn't very good at getting up and my father used to get quite angry 'If you don't get up I'll come and get you up'. Anyhow I was very successful, although I still found it very hard to get up so early. But I loved it... We had eight paperboys and if one of them didn't turn up I had to go out and deliver very early in the morning. We had a little pony and so I used to go out and make the deliveries on the pony."*

As a child Mollie Muetzel knew the shop well. *"Wards the sweet shop was down Lord Street where I used to have to go and buy my father's cigarettes - I had a shilling and I got a halfpenny change for twenty Players. Those were the days! And I used to spend it usually, so it was always a run to the sweet shop."*

Drury Brothers menswear and E Ward's newsagents (1963)

By 1936 Miss Ward had opened a second shop here in the High Street where she sold calendars, writing sets, greetings cards and 'fancy stationery'. She also offered 'early delivery of daily and Sunday newspapers, magazines and periodicals'. *"I moved into the shop in the High Street as I thought it would give me more business – which it did. But I kept the shop in Lord Street and got someone else to run it for me. I had a very good girl and I was able to leave her. One of the people who worked for me, she's now died but her husband Roy still comes to see me... My brother lived with us above the shop but later he got married and I lived there on my own."*

In the 1930s it was rare to find women running their own shops – and there was only one other lady running a business in Hoddesdon at that time: Mrs Mitchell at the Hoddesdon Bazaar. *"She had a paper shop like me, but later she sold hers. We were rivals, but we got on very well. Being in business we knew all the shopkeepers. I was a member of the Chamber of Commerce and we used to meet the other business owners."*

Joan Umney was a regular customer in the 1940s. *"Miss Ward was a very smart lady. I think the counters were at the side and I think she put money into a drawer. I know I used to come up the town and get the paper... There used to be the cough candy – you could buy that in a long bit, or she would break it up for you – dolly mixtures, little sweets always in the great big jars. She put them into little papers bags – weighed them out in funny little scales."*

Hedley Eariss was employed by Miss Ward in the 1950s. *" I started work when I was 13 as a paperboy, and then at 15 getting the rounds together in the early morning in the shop."* Les Riches was a customer in the same era. *"We used to go into the sweet shop and buy a few sweets and our coconut tobacco – it was shredded coconut which was covered in chocolate which looked like tobacco, that was the era when most people used to smoke, and sherbet dabs, sweet cigarettes, flying saucers, that sort of thing".* In 1963 the business moved a few doors further up the High Street to number 103 where it still bears Miss Ward's name today, despite having had a number of different owners over the last few decades.

Tina retired to live at St David's Drive in Broxbourne, relishing the long lie-ins that she'd never been able to enjoy for the previous half century. She is currently living in a nursing home at Stanstead Abbotts where she has been since 2008. Her final recommendation is: *"If you go into business don't take a newsagent – take an old woman's advice – anything but a newsagent! It's early mornings seven days a week. The only time I got off was Christmas Day and Boxing Day, and how I longed for that! If I had my time again, I wouldn't do it. How glad I was to get rid of it."*

THE WHITE SWAN (95, High Street) currently the same

The White Swan was built in the late 16th century when Hoddesdon already had 30 inns or alehouses with beer brewed on the premises in a prosperous settlement of around 130 dwellings. Unlike most of its contemporaries, this hostelry has kept pretty much the same name for over 400 years - having also been known as the Swan or Old Swan at various times. Tregelles reports: *"This belonged from early times to the Sharnbrook family , who held it until 1600 or a little later, when it passed into the hands of John Bailey, gentleman, who married a Sharnbrook heiress, and was the owner of a good many other houses... The smithy adjoining once belonged to the Thurgoods, and apparently then stood detached on Hoddesdon Green before the Inn was built."*

West side of High Street from the Bull Hotel to the White Swan (1920s)

In 1891 Fanny Collins, a 45year old widow, was running the inn. Her six year old daughter Caroline, a servant and a lodger also lived there with her. By the end of the century William Nix was listed as the landlord and George Reed, wheelwright, was based in his back yard.

W.G. Nicholls set up as a butcher in a small shop in the north end of the building during the 19th century. In the 1890s it is being run by William 'Billy' Nicholls who was Captain of the Fire Brigade and, according to Paddick, *"a man with a frightening way of talking but behind all that he had a heart of gold, and did many kindnesses by stealth."*

Michael Dear reveals, *"my mother went in there as a live-in house maid, and she worked there until she got married. Because she used to work in the butchers and made all the sausages, she had the secret recipe of the sausages. And she told Billy Nicholls that she'd keep that recipe a secret 'til the day she died. People used to ask her what was in these sausages, and she used to say 'a little bit of this and a little bit of that', but she never did actually give the recipe away."*

By the 1920s Nicholls had moved to Burford Street and their premises had been taken over by Ripley's butchers who, in turn, re-located to the building next door in 1963 allowing the shop space to become initially an off license and later to be re-incorporated into the pub itself. Pevsner

The White Swan (c1900) with Billy Nicholl's butcher's shop on the right

describes the tavern in his 1953 Hertfordshire volume of *The Buildings of England* as *"visually the most striking timber-framed inn in the district."*

R J RIPLEY BUTCHER (99, High Street) currently the same

We only have to take a few steps and we can examine one of the town's oldest properties. This was originally the location of Hoddesdon's smithy which had been operating here for centuries. Henry Giblin was the farrier and smith in 1891, succeeded by W H Mumford by 1900, with W H Saward and Son offering *'Practical Shoeing and General Smiths'* from the same premises just before the First World War.

George Henry Porter was the last owner of the forge and ran the business through the 1920s into the 1930s having previously been a farrier for the powder mills at Enfield and at Christie's brewery. Mary Newton was fascinated with the place as a child. *"I can remember coming home from school and spending hours hanging over the door, watching him shoe horses, I shall never forget the smell of the burning as they fitted the shoe."*

Having moved to the south end of this property over 50 years ago, Ripley's still remains in business as the town's only surviving butcher.

TEA ROOM + DESTE PHOTOGRAPHIC STUDIO (101, High Street) currently Attitudes Hair & Beauty

Mr E W Stagg set up his boot makers in the centre of this tenement in the late 19th century, moving across to the opposite side of the road in 1905 where his son continued the business until the 1970s. *(see page 135)* During the 1930s the upstairs rooms became the meeting place or 'everyman's house', for a local Toc H branch which was a social club and fellowship group for ex-servicemen. In the *Journal* in 1947 it advertised its events programme: *'Wednesday Night Club Night: Lectures, Discussions, Music, Drama, etc. Refreshments.'* By 1963 the building also housed a cafe, photographer's studio and a chiropodist's practice.

WARD'S NEWSAGENTS (103, High Street) currently still is

Baker and confectioner Frederick 'Freddy' Scott ran the Excelsior Bakery here in the last quarter of the 19th century which was famous for its halfpenny buns, according to Edward Paddick. The business had changed its name to H W Johnson Bakers by 1935, advertising themselves as: *'Fancy Bread & Biscuit Baker. Wedding and Birthday cakes to order'*. By the mid 1950s D W Reynolds Jewellers have their shop here, before moving round into Lord Street in 1963 to make way for Miss Ward's newsagent.

THE SALISBURY (105, High Street) currently closed, awaiting re-fit

We now move on the town's third surviving ancient tavern. The Salisbury started life back in the early 16th century as the Star when, Tregelles reports *"it was, with an adjoining house and 69 acres of land, the property of John Borrell, Serjeant-at Arms to Henry VIII. A star was the badge of the De Veres, Earls of Oxford, who in 1303 held Goldingtons manor (now Hailey Hall)."* This direct connection of a landlord to the Tudor monarch may possibly explain the story relating to the 'king's saddle' at the Golden Lion. *(see page 7)*

The inn appears to have been re-named 'The Blake Lyon' (Black Lion) some time prior to 1578 when it features under that title in a court roll. The old Court House believed to have been built by the Earl of Salisbury in 1610 was on the north side of the inn. The medieval Manor Court continued to meet there until 1826 when, Tregelles informs us, it had become *"a mere excuse for eating and drinking; hot halfpence were thrown to be scrambled for, and altogether it was a source of disorder."*

The north end of the High Street with the Salisbury on the left (c1890s)

Hayllar adds: *"at the rear was a great range of stabling with a cockpit, and behind this again, a bowling green."*

The place attracted a very upmarket clientele according to a 1638 letter sent by Sir Edward Baeshe, which reported, *"Lord Newburgh and Sir Thos. Littleton dined and sent for my cousin Elrington, who won some of their money at bowls."* This probably accounts for the names given to some of its guest rooms such as 'the King's Room' and 'the painted parlour'. It was re-fronted in smart red brick some time in the 18th century. It had its name changed again to its present one in the early 19th century – its sign was the last of the three spanning the road to survive, being removed in 1875.

The tenants in the early 19th century were the Batty family famous for both their ales and silver tankards. According to Tregelles, *"it was for years the custom of the maltmen of Hertford, who had been attending Hoddesdon market, to gather afterwards at the Black Lion, wait there until the last of them was come in and then start as a body to ride home. Hertford Heath was then so infested with thieves that travellers thus banded together for mutual defence."* Later in the century the Brewster family became tenants and managed the inn until 1868. By the late 1890s George Gibson is the landlord. In the first half of the 20th century a poultry market was held in a yard at the rear. *(see page 131)*

The Hoddesdon Whippet Racing Club outside the Salisbury (1922)

The function room was hired out to all manner of local organisations and societies, presumably to the likes of the Hoddesdon Whippet Racing Club featured in this delightful photo *(above)* from the 1920s. Many locals celebrated weddings, birthdays, anniversaries and other memorable events there - Valerie Bateman was one of them. *"When we got married in 1957 we looked into other places to have our wedding reception, but the Salisbury was big enough for the number of people we had. In those days you didn't have masses of people to your wedding – we had about 50. And they did us a really good meal there."*

The hostelry was unexpectedly bought by the Wetherspoons pub chain at the end of 2013 and has been closed for nearly nine months pending major internal refurbishment work.

GAS BOARD OFFICES (109, High Street) currently Zagara Restaurant

Paddick tells us that the first building on this site was *"a large house of two storeys having at its south end an east facing gable; the whole building had been cement rendered. In 1860 it was protected along the High Street by four pillars having a two foot wall between them, and a hedge behind the wall... The house stood about 24ft back from the footpath."*

By the late 19th century it had become a *'printer and fancy stationer'* run by William Clark and his son William Jnr, which was subsequently bought by Thomas Knight who moved the firm down to the east side of the High Street around 1920. *(see page 143)* In the 1930s an unsightly square extension had been tacked across one half of the facade for the convenience of its new owners: the Tottenham Gas Company.

The large old house was demolished in 1959 and a new showroom and offices were built for the Eastern Gas Board by local firm Haward's – Michael Dear was one of the construction team.

MYDDELTON HOUSE

This impressive house was built around 1620 as a private residence, and may have been the home of William Myddleton, Elizabethan poet, naval adventurer, and brother of Sir Hugh Myddelton who constructed the New River. By the early 18th century it had become an inn called the Queens Head and stayed as such until 1852. By the late 19th century it had become home to Charles Augustus Christie, one of the sons of the owner of the brewery opposite. *(see page 122)* It subsequently became the residence and surgery of local GP, Dr Love who was succeeded by Dr Leonard West, until he re-located to Rathmore House at the southern end of the town. *(see page 164)* By the mid 1930s the ground floor has been split into three separate retail units. One was occupied in 1936 by

Myddleton House (c1890s)

bookmakers, John Scott Turf & Football Accountant, promising '*Extra Generous Odds and Prompt Payment.*'

OWEN'S CHEMISTS (113, High Street) currently The Tan House

Local Estate Agents, Flower & Swift were based at number 113 in the late 1930s. Some twenty years later this has become the location of Owen's chemists, who had a second branch in Rye Road. By the 1980s the Gold Shop is based here.

FUNERAL PARLOUR (115, High Street) currently EFE Supermarket

Taplin Brothers, House Furnishers & Cabinet Makers moved here in 1938. In 1963 this was home to a funeral parlour that was later replaced by a branch of Milletts who had re-located here by the 1980s.

FORDHAM'S PRAMS (117, High Street) currently Herts Plaice

In 1936 the Modern Stores opened with the bold claim: '*The Money*

Myddleton House (1963)

Saving Stores are Here! Let us help you with your weekly outlay. Money buys more with us.' A decade later Wilsons of Enfield had a General Builders Merchants operating here at number 117 - by 1955 they had in turn been superseded by a drapers shop run by J Stanford-Thomas. In the early 1960s the Fordham family had set up a shop on this site to sell prams and baby goods separately from their furniture store opposite. *(see page 119)* Previous to that, according to Joan Umney, customers who wanted to buy prams had to visit the company's furniture store over in Hertford to view the stock. In the 1980s BJs are running a cafe here.

DOUGLAS H MILLAR OPTICIAN (119, High Street)

By the 1930s a rather basic single storey extension had been thrown up on the north side of Myddleton House and housed two new retail units. In 1936 independent optician Douglas Millar is encouraging locals to have their eyes tested. *'Headaches – Sore Lids – Aching Eyes – are common symptoms of eye strain.'* By the early 1960s the business is now owned and run as a branch of the Clement Clarke chain. Modes boutique is installed here in the 1980s.

HITCHING'S SHOE SHOP (121, High Street)

In the 1890s Thomas George Hitching was listed as a 'shoe dealer' in Rye Road, but in 1936 the family re-located to this premises and became a rival to the Carter's well-established shoe shop further down the street. Competition between the two retailers really heated up during the 1960s with both taking out full page adverts every month in the *Journal* featuring the ever-changing, seasonal footwear fashions of that era.

At some point towards the end of the twentieth century the lean-to extension was extended to a second storey and now blends in unobtrusively with its host, albeit to the detriment of the original building's architectural symmetry.

AMWELL STREET

It is at this point that we pass the northern extent of the High Street and deliberately continue on into Amwell Street - originally known as Ware Valley as it featured a steep hill descending out of the town. A serious accident in the early 1820s led to approaches being made to one of the town's most prominent citizens – the renowned road engineer, James McAdam *(see page 160)* - who recommended the reduction in the gradient. Remedial works carried out in 1826 created the 'High Path', which was also later called 'The Rise'. Amazingly this feature still survives today on the eastern side of the road, despite the massive re-development of this end of the town in the last half century.

SAMS & BRYANTS (1, Amwell St)

Our first stop here is not a building but an entrance way that led down to a builder's yard run by another old established family business: Sams & Bryants. In 1935 their advert in the Journal re-assures potential customers of their bona fides. *'Decorators, Plumbers & Hot Water Fitters, repairs and alterations carefully executed by experienced workmen and all work personally supervised.* '

C J ROSS (3-9, Amwell St) currently Johnson Ross Fishing Tackle

This was the location of the Old Harrow pub which prominently advertised the use of a public telephone in 1899. Mr Page set up a forage

C J Ross & Son and Brewster Brothers (1963)

store here, which was taken over around 1905 by C J Ross & Son who had an existing branch in Broxbourne. Mr Ross was Honorary Treasurer of the Hoddesdon Swimming Club in the 1920s which held regular Swimming Galas at the indoor brewery baths in Bell Lane. *(see page 123)*

The company was also a 'Domestic Fuel Merchants' according to a 1935 advert. *'We are noted for coke throughout the district. All grades suitable for domestic boilers, ovens and coke fires in stock for immediate delivery.'* George Don's family bought their coal from the local supplier. *"He used to come round with this flat truck and a horse and this old boy used to sit on the back with his legs dangling. And they had this whacking big hundredweight metal weight on top of the empty bags. And a lovely smell there was. When they got to your house they wouldn't go round the back – they used to tramp through the house with a bag of coal on their shoulders and shoot it out the back in the shed."*

Dorothy Chilton visited the shop regularly. *"They sold animal feeds and, of course, fishing gear. They had sacks of corn and different wheat and that sort of thing – they had shovels and put the amount you wanted in bags. We always had chickens and rabbits in the back garden, and bought dog biscuits – the boneos."* But even animal feed was rationed during the war, as George Don recalls. *"You used to have a ration card and you were allowed so much chicken meal a week depending on how many chickens you had – we had about half a dozen. And it used to be my job to come up to town and get the chicken meal on Saturday."*

Alan Cook confirms that son and heir, Ronnie Ross, appears to have inherited his father's passion for water sports and was a well known face at the Open Air Swimming Pool in the 1950s and 60s. *"Another character of the town was Ronnie Ross, and he and some other people there, they were running the Water Polo team and that used to be quite an enjoyable thing on a Friday evening."* Fellow trader Brian Walsh from Meadows also knew Ronnie in the post-war period. *"I used to do a bit of fishing at one time and so I used to buy a bit of gear from him. Always an interesting character – he loved to chat, and I like to chat as well. And I used to say 'I've got to go now Ronnie,' and so he'd say 'All right, then – bugger off, if you must'."*

Today the Ross family name has survived on the facade of their old shop which is now enormously successful as a specialist fishing tackle retailer. A few years back the business expanded their premises into the whole adjoining property after it had undergone a major renovation.

Shoe Repairers (1963)

The adjacent property is called Amwell Terrace and was put up in 1884 – before that a row of three cottages dating back to about 1600 stood there. In the 1930s the building housed the Surplus Supply Stores which boasted the *'Largest Shoe Stores In The District - Wellingtons And House Shoes Always In Stock.'* as well as *'Ladies, Gent's and Children's Complete Outfits: No Fancy Prices at These Stores.'*

In the post war period their premises was split into three separate units and by the early 1960s the Brewster's are operating their Fishmongers shop at number 5. Next door at number 7 was a shoe repairer, while number 9 was the entrance to a private flat above their shop. The end unit was a butchers shop for many years in the first half of the twentieth century kept by the two Bowden brothers and later by Mr Leach, before being adapted to serve as the town's first telephone exchange. It had become the home of Floral Wise in the 1980s, which traded there for some 20 years.

PAUL'S LANE

If we'd been hurrying past this corner before the late 1980s we'd probably have missed the narrow alley if we'd blinked. Prior to the 19th century this had been known as Jordan's Lane, Westfield Lane and Goodman's Lane at various times. By the time the first school was set up here in 1844 it had become Paul's Lane - possibly named after a local family working as blacksmiths during the 18th century at 'Hoddesdon End'.

HODDESDON PARISH CHURCH

For hundreds of years worshipping in Hoddesdon was a somewhat divisive affair due to the unfortunate fact that the town was split unevenly between the two competing parishes of Great Amwell and Broxbourne, causing a certain amount of rather un-Christian quarrelling. In 1732 Robert Plomer, who ran a profitable local brewery in the town, was in dispute for some reason with the Vicar of Broxbourne, Phineas Rothwell, and built a 'chapel of ease' for himself just to the west of the ruins of the old Chapel of St Katherine at the north end of the High Street. As Percy Gandon puts it in *The House of My Pilgrimage*, his history of the Parish Church published in 1976, *"it was certainly an unusual step to build what was in effect a private chapel, but accords with the character of this self-made man for whom money meant power."*

After Plomer's death in 1742 the chapel fell into disuse and it wasn't until the early 1820s that moves were made to raise the money by public subscription to purchase it. In 1823 the current owner, Captain Hugh Hughes, sold the building to the town. It was consecrated on 8th July by the Bishop of London as 'The Chapel of Hoddesdon'. Due to the fact that it was situated on the border between the Great Amwell and Broxbourne parishes it was agreed that the right of presentation should alternate between their vicars.

Hoddesdon finally became a parish in its own right in 1843 when, as Tregelles reports, *"a district containing about 1700 inhabitants of the parish of Broxbourne and 500 from the parish of Great Amwell was assigned to the church by the order of the Queen in Council under an Act of George III."* The new 'Consolidated Chapelry District of Hoddesdon' came into being on 2nd January 1844 *"for the purpose of affording accommodation for attending divine service to the persons resident in the said district... and the preservation and improvement of the moral habits of the persons resident therein."*

By 1860 the chapel was considered too small to accommodate all the parishioners in the newly expanded congregation and an open meeting

Hoddesdon Chapel (c1825)

was called to discuss building a new, larger church, but only five people turned up. Ambitious plans for raising enough money for a completely new building floundered on for several years until an architect was appointed to provide plans to enlarge the existing chapel *'for purposes of public worship and the convenience and comfort of the congregation be considered… that the ornament be simple… and limited in cost.'*

A chancel, the base of a bell tower and two porches, one to the west and another to the south, were built in 1865 by local builder John Hunt who was also a churchwarden. The tower and spire were completed in 1887 thanks to a bequest by William East. The new Parish Church only had two serving vicars for its first 78 years: Rev Richard Morice (1843 – 1881) and Re. Philip Esme Stewart Holland (1881- 1921). At the end of the 19th century the Rev Holland was holding daily services at 11am and 6.30pm.

The church was originally known as St. Catherine's and, despite the strange disappearance of the vestry records from the late 19th century, it is named as such on contemporary maps and in Trade Directories of the late Victorian period. When a new set of bells were presented by the five sons of Charles Peter Christie in memory of their parents and a grand brass lectern was donated by the Christie daughters a dedication took place in 1901 where the Rev Holland decided to change the name to St. Paul's.

According to Percy Gandon, *"it is reasonably clear why this name was chosen. Some people were doubtful of saints other than those found in the bible, and there are indications that this kind of tradition existed in Hoddesdon at that time. The choice of St Paul was no doubt suggested by the name of the small lane at the side of the church and school."* After a major restoration and modernisation programme in 1976, Gandon tells us: *"the threads of the confused and curious past were drawn together and Hoddesdon Parish Church became 'St Catherine and St Paul'."*

Peter Shepherd earned extra pocket money from his church attendance in the 1930s: *"I was a choir boy in the parish church for a number of years... You would go to choir practice about twice a week in the evenings, and then you would attend church Sunday mornings, and sing hymns in the evening. And plus, of course, any wedding that was going on, if they wanted you.... We got paid for weddings - not too much, I would think it's probably something like sixpence - but that was worth having in those days."*

Parish Church of St Catherine and St Paul exterior (c1900)

His contemporary Mollie Muetzel admits to not being very devout in her teenage devotions. *"I was told to go to the English church, and I'm afraid we didn't enjoy that nearly as much. Betty and I, when we used to go on a Sunday morning, we used to take little games to play up in the balcony - but we'd been to church! Well, we didn't like the vicar very much - he was called 'Tootsie'... But we found it a bit boring, I'm afraid."*

THE HOME FRONT IN HODDESDON

Standing here next to the church seems an appropriate place to take a break to talk about the event that probably had more impact, for good or ill, on all the citizens of Hoddesdon than any other in its thousand year history – the Second World War. *(see pages 195-207)* It was only a few hundred yards from where we are standing that the town's only fatalities were recorded in the bombing raid of 10th May 1941.*(see page 13)*

Peter Shepherd lived in Paul's Lane and was an eyewitness. *"A series of bombs fell, one of which hit the house next door but one to us, and unfortunately killed two people there - one a little evacuee, my friend, who was eleven years old and had been evacuated from Stratford. And sadly he was killed together with the 19-year-old son of the homeowner, Mrs Stevenson. That was quite a nasty experience. I certainly remember the night quite clearly where all the ARP, fire engines, ambulances came down the lane and suddenly someone called for complete quiet while they were examining - they'd obviously found the bodies and were examining them to see whether they were alive or not. Sadly they didn't survive."*

Everyone who was a child on the fateful autumn Sunday when war was declared in September 1939 still has vivid memories of exactly where they were and what they were doing. Mary Newton was shelling peas in the garden. *"I was 12 years old at the time, but I do remember it, because almost immediately afterwards, the air raid siren went and everyone rushed out to their front gates. But it was nothing at all, but I think everyone got into a bit of a panic."* Olive Knight was absolutely terrified. *"I can remember screaming - because the siren went and I thought terrible things were going to happen. There was an air raid shelter that had already been built down beside the council offices, and we went over there... I was eleven."*

The country was immediately put on to a war footing and soon evacuees began to be sent out of the cities. In the *Journal* chief reporter, 'Onlooker', made a plea to his fellow townspeople: *"Let me act the gentleman I certainly am in my better moments by extending greetings to these evacuees from the Metropolis. May the old town provide hospitable sanctuary for them, and may they leave the town as they find it – or, if possible, just a little better off for their stay amongst us."*

Joan Umney was one of those new arrivals in 1940 – she was just three when her fireman father was killed during the bombing of the docks. *"When we came from London first of all we lived in Stortford Road with my mum's sister because we had nowhere to live. And then we moved to my other Auntie who lived in Burford Street... And she went down to North Road and knocked on Mrs Duff's door who had six children and she asked her 'I wonder if you could let out a couple of your rooms?' So we lived in two rooms - my mum and my sister and I – and we had to walk to Belcher Road round the back because the toilet was out in the garden. And we had our water in a bucket, we had the coal up one corner and an oil stove on top of a little cupboard."*

Cyril Phelps was sent up from Tottenham to stay with his mother's two sisters in Nazeing, *"for safety reasons. That was fortunate, because they bombed our house shortly after that. So, as luck would have it, we weren't in the house at the time. But this stay in Nazeing became a longer period of time than we'd envisioned. I was due to start Nazeing School on Monday morning, but it was firebombed on the Friday and we finished up doing about two mornings a week in a Chapel Hall. Hence I lost a lot of schooling."*

A disrupted education was something that a whole wartime generation of children were to experience, even in rural Hoddesdon. *"We only used to go to school three days a week, because the evacuees came from London, you see,"* explains Michael Dear. *"Because we were only a small village school, of course, there wasn't enough room for all of us. So we went Mondays, Wednesdays and Fridays, and they went Tuesdays, Thursdays and Saturdays, and Sunday mornings."*

Then there were the constant air raid warnings during the school day, as Peter Shepherd remembers: *"there were a series of zigzag air raid shelters built underground, covered with soil. And you just carried an exercise book, I think, and went down - no lighting in them at all - sat in the shelter until the all clear went, when you filed back to school again. You were probably only there a few minutes before the siren went again, and you repeated that same process and this went on several times a day on many occasions, so really you didn't get too many lessons in."*

PAUL'S LANE SCHOOLS

And the school Peter is talking about was located here in the single storey red brick buildings on the right hand side of Paul's Lane by the church.

An Endowed National School for Girls was founded on the east side of Amwell Street in 1818 by Mrs Easter Jones, who also provided an annual income of £30.00. A contemporary record specified the premises should be used as *"a school house for the teaching of so many poor girls, children of persons belonging to the hamlet of Hoddesdon, as Trustees should think fit to be taught therein to spell, knit and work at their needle."*

In 1858 the school moved into newly built premises adjacent to the Parish Church where a Boys' National School had been set up in 1844 thanks to a successful fund-raising campaign by Rev R W Morice, first vicar of St Catherine's. The boys' building accommodated 225 children and an infants' school large enough to take 150 pupils was also built, alongside the Master's House. At the turn of the 20th century Miss Helen Welch was headmistress of the Girls' School overseeing an impressive average attendance of 117, while Mr W J Fowler served as Head of the Boys' School from 1871 to his retirement in 1913.

Head of the Boys' School, Mr Fowler (centre), with school staff (c1900)

In his book Edward Paddick paints an evocative picture of his Edwardian schooldays. *"The games played... were hoops, peg and whip tops, two kinds of games with marbles, one demanding a scooped out hole at the base of a fence or wall, and the other played along the road. A game called five stones was introduced towards the end of my period at school, and various games were played with cigarette cards, which were avidly collected by most of the boys. The game played with conkers occupied us for a few weeks in the autumn, and many tricks were used to make them hard such as baking them, soaking them in beer, or applying oil to them. This practice was most unsporting and severely frowned upon."*

Mrs. Giles was appointed Headmistress of the Infants in 1916 by school managers who included Robert Barclay, Major O F Christie and Mrs Festing Bryant. She retired in August 1936 after 50 years in the teaching profession. She told the *Journal* about the vast changes she'd witnessed in her career and concluded: *"Children nowadays… are becoming more self-reliant and have greater opportunities of advancement than was the case years ago."*

In 1930 the older pupils moved to the newly completed Senior County Council School in Burford Street. Peter Shepherd, living in Paul's Lane, didn't have far to go to the infant school in the 1930s: *"the school was some ten yards from my gateway. From five until eleven – classes were roughly 30 people, as far as I can recall."* Mary Newton was another pupil at that time: *"St Paul's School had no facilities at all... I can remember we used to have great open fires in the classrooms, and we used to put our bottles of milk in front of it to get hot when we had our break."*

Joan Umney started there during the war. *"It was a very old building; we had the little wooden desks with inkwells and that sort of thing. And the teachers were obviously very strict – you were frightened – whereas nowadays, well…it's changed. I remember Mr Parker – he was very smart and very tall and dark-suited. We had a big blackboard at the front. And they used to fill one blackboard and then turn it over and fill the other side. Not that we had a sports field – we only played games in the playground, because the playground was quite big. We used to skip, play hopscotch."* Because they were orphans who had been evacuated Joan and her sister were entitled to free lunches. *"So we used to walk back down to North Road – and on that road there was what they used to call 'The*

Playtime at the school (1968)

Institute' and we used to go there and have a meal. And I can remember mum – she was there every day at the door when we came out to wave to us as we went back off to school."

After the end of the Second World War boys and girls were taught together in mixed classes. In April 1953 the juniors moved to Burford Street School after the opening of the new Secondary School in Stanstead Road. The infants finally moved to the newly re-named Haslewood School in 1971. Not long afterwards the school buildings at the east end of the site were pulled down to facilitate the widening of Paul's Lane

PAUL WALLACE ESTATE AGENT (20, Amwell Street) currently Morrisons

We now retrace our steps back to the High Street where opposite us on the High Path in the late 1950s we would have seen a pretty row of old cottages, one housing the office of an estate agency run by Paul Wallace. The business had been set up in 1949 with wife Molly as secretary looking after the office while Paul went off to appointments on his push bike. In 1954 Stanley Vaughan joined and later became Office Manager.

Amwell Street looking North with the old rectory on left and the high pavement on right (c1900)

Having tried a few different jobs, by 1959 local lad Peter Haynes had not yet found a career he really wanted to follow. *"One day I fortunately saw an advertisement in the local paper: 'Mr Paul Wallace seeking young man to join estate agency – no previous experience necessary, but willing to work hard, etc, etc.' Well, my uncle was also an Estate Agent - Herbert Haynes & Co - who was well known in Hoddesdon in the pre and post war years. So that had given me some basic training and a basic interest in that business."*

Peter was fortunate enough to be called for an interview. *"I was a very lucky man – Paul Wallace decided I was the right boy for the job and gave me the job. And he said, 'Do you want to train as a Chartered Surveyor, Peter, or do you just want to work at it and sell?' And I said, 'I'm more of a salesman, Mr Wallace.' And he said, 'Jolly good!' He was a charming man, Paul Wallace. And he gave me the job and I never looked back."*

Peter went on to work his way up in the business – after a move to the 'Old Cottage' at the southern end of the town necessitated by the building of the Tower Centre he was made a partner in the firm. The company expanded in the 1960s and 70s, opened several other branches and a commercial arm only to have to retrench in the recession of the mid 70s.

In 1980 Paul Wallace retired and Peter became sole director of the agency, joined by that same year by his son Neil. The 80s were boom years with further expansion into various areas of operation, until once again recession hit the sector very hard. Peter managed to steer the business through the next turbulent decade successfully before handing over to Neil and taking a well-earned retirement in 2000. Although he still keeps a watching brief as a consultant based in the Cottage.

NORRIS' BIKE & RADIO SHOP (16, Amwell Street) currently The Pavilion

Two doors further along in the direction of the town before 1965 we would have seen the original location of another of Hoddesdon's well established family businesses. This was a bicycle and radio store, which later sold motorbikes and electrical goods, run by the Norris family. Malcolm Norris who was the last owner of the business tells how his father first started back in the 1930s.

"My father came from Ordnance Road, Enfield where he worked with his father - my grandfather - and they were a cycle, motorcycle and car chauffeur business. There were seven brothers and my father left home - as all the brothers did - and set up his own business in Hoddesdon in 1931... He set up in a very small way and he didn't have any money – he was 17 years old. It must have been so difficult. He always told me he almost lived on stale cakes because he could get those easily. That was the sort of life it was. "

Mr Norris senior built up the business, married a Cheshunt girl called Ellaline, and was making enough money to be able to purchase 16, Amwell Street. The family moved into this old three storey building to live above the shop with his mother, and Malcolm was born in 1939. Whilst many small shops sold a range of products - as we have noted previously - the combination of motorbikes and electrical items does seem to be rather an odd one, but it clearly worked.

"Everything went well until the war came along and then my father was taken in to work at Nazeing Aerodrome where he was an engine mechanic, engineer, and he looked after all the light aircraft that came in there. It wasn't warplanes, but all the planes associated with the war. My mother came into the business then and ran the business while he was away."

Norris' Radio & Cycles shop in the 1930s

Over the twenty years after the war the whole Norris family worked very hard and prospered, with Malcolm now at his father's side. By the time he reached 18, Les Riches could wait no longer to buy his own machine which he'd admired in Norris' window, but he didn't have enough money. *"So I said to my dad 'Can you lend me the money?' £183 it was – a Francis Barnett motorbike. Scooters and motorbikes were all the rage in the 60s. And the guy who was the manager of the motorcycle section, he was a tall chap and he lived in Stortford Road, and he delivered my new motorbike home to me – he rode it down for me. No crash helmet in those days and I jumped on and went haring off down Rye Road."*

By the early 1960s the Norris' business had expanded and was thriving. They had modernised their premises, bought three cottages so they owned a whole strip of land across to Burford Street, and had built a large motorcycle workshop at the rear employing six mechanics. Suddenly in 1962 a large developer, the Heron Group, approached Hoddesdon Urban District Council with a proposal to build a massive shopping precinct which involved buying up all the properties in the triangle of land at the top of the High Street.

Ariel shot of the north end of Hoddesdon showing the 'triangle' which was to be demolished to make way for the Tower Centre (c1950s)

Malcolm describes his father's immediate reaction: *"It's my freehold; it's my life that I've spent building this business to what it is. I have just completely rebuilt the whole site, right the way through to the workshops, garages at the back - everything."* The last thing Stanley Norris wanted to do was sell. *"But it was pressure, pressure, pressure - until we were told that, unless we came to an agreement, it would be a compulsory purchase order. Because the Council with the Heron Group - and whether the Government had been approached at that time I don't know - they decided it was going to go ahead whether we liked it or not."*

THE TOWER CENTRE

The first many residents of Hoddesdon knew of the grand plan to change the face of their town was a brief article in the June 1962 edition of the *Hoddesdon Journal* headlined: '*Scheme for Re-developing Town Centre Disclosed*'. *"The Town Planning Committee reported the receipt of a letter from a firm of architects and engineers which stated that a planning application was shortly to be made... Councillor Jones said that the proposal was made by a firm which probably had not the remotest idea of Hoddesdon and what it stands for. The proposal showed the intention of sweeping away everything in the area north of the clock and possibly even the Clock Tower itself."*

Within a mere couple of months, during which time there was no formal public consultation, the detailed proposals for a modern block of shops with flats immediately above on the three acre site were being put forward for approval. At a meeting on August 29th the Hoddesdon UDC accepted a recommendation by their Planning Committee to grant outline planning permission for the scheme which was estimated to cost about £500,000. In September 1962 the *Journal* reported: *"Mr Gerald Ronson, a Director of the Heron group of companies, said that a shopping centre of the type envisaged by this scheme should pull in trade from surrounding districts. It would, too, encourage Hoddesdon people to stay in the town to do their shopping, instead of going to other towns as they do now."*

Malcolm Norris, with understandable bitterness, recalls: *"Because it was going to be a modern pedestrianised centre – that was almost unique in this country. It was the time of modern development and the Tower Centre plans were presented to us as 'God's gift to Hoddesdon,' without any doubt at all. And to a certain extent we all went along with what was expected."*

According to Peter Shepherd, locals were shocked by the speed with which this development was foisted on the town. *" It was something that they didn't really know too much about, it was decided by the Council and other interested parties - I don't know the real reason why, I don't think anyone will ever really know. But obviously the old buildings: the old Clock Tower, the old Clock House Garage and the Maidenhead pub were such nice features and to tear them down and replace them with the monstrosity that's there at the moment, to me is completely wrong."*

The Maidenhead Inn

The old hostelry and timber-clad garage next to it greatly contributed to the character of our traditional market town. This area was originally the site of an ancient manor house owned by Richard de Boxe dating back to 1256. Tregelles informs us *"The enclosure where this stood was called Culverhouse Croft, and the site of the manor was held by the payment of 'a red rose at the nativity of St John the Baptist' (midsummer day)."* The Maidenhead almost certainly dated back to Queen Elizabeth I's reign - its name refers to the Virgin Queen. The earliest it appears in a document is 1576, although there had been a house there since the 14th century. It was the property of the Thorowgood family until 1622, when it was acquired by Marmaduke Rawdon as part of his marriage settlement.

Sydney Staines, last landlord of the Maidenhead with his wife just prior to the building's demolition (1964)

George Don only ventured into the pub once when he was home on leave from the army. *"There were two bars – the public bar on the left and the other one. You never went in the other one, the saloon bar. As far as I remember it was very dingy, I don't exactly remember the décor but it was all dark. And I remember half way up the walls was wood all the way round. There was one of those skittle games in the corner and possibly a dart board, but there wasn't billiards and those sorts of things. It had a brass rail round the bottom of the bar – to put your feet on. It seemed to be all old boys in there, all standing up, all had macs on. And it was straight-sided glasses in them days, the place was full of smoke – everyone was lighting these pipes up – it smelt like a bonfire. I was smoking myself in them days and so you didn't think anything of it."*

Clock House Garage

An ancient timber framed tenement split into two separate residences was on this corner for hundreds of years before being demolished in 1875 and

The Clock House Garage (1963)

replaced by a distinctive timber clad building which housed the town's public bathhouse. By the early 1930s it had become Austin's Garage, which in June 1935 was re-named Rye House Garage presumably to reflect new ownership. It offered *"everything for the motorist"* from *"finest grades of oil and petrol supplied from modern electric pumps with speed, efficiency and civility"*, repairs and servicing for private and commercial vehicles, plus car hire.

It was later re-branded yet again as the Clock House Garage. Les Riches filled up his motorcycle there every week. *"I just used to pull up outside the pumps and the chap used to come out and I used to have my shots of two stroke oil in the tank and my 4/6d worth of petrol and shake the bike about to mix it up."*

Re-development

Michael Dear remembers the major demolition works that began in 1964. *"We worked on the new Gas Showrooms which is right opposite the Clock Tower. Of course, while we were building that, they were demolishing all where the Tower Centre is now. All the High Paths were uprooted, and all the lovely old trees that used to be there, they were all bulldozed down."*

Demolition of Paul Wallace Estate Agents on the left and Norris' shop on the right.

In January 1965 the *Hoddesdon Journal* revealed: *'Plans for the Heron Group's Shopping Development betwixt Amwell Street and Burford Street have at last been finalised. Now it is – Action Stations!'* Regular updates followed, accompanied by photographs of the building works in progress. *(pages 96-7)* In June 1966 work on the project was reported as proceeding to programme, with the cost having already doubled to £1m. *"To date over 900 tons of steel and 10,000 cubic yards of concrete have been placed in position in the structure. Operatives were surprised by an outcrop of coal discovered about 25 ft down at the south end of the site during excavations."*

In October of that year the precinct's architect told the paper *"The pedestrian courts in the development are to be treated in an interesting and artistic manner, and landscaping will be carried out as far as it practicable, including special lighting and seating to give pleasant surroundings in which shopping can be done in comfort."*

But, according to Malcolm Norris, the glossy plans were never implemented in full. *"There are some things that were drawn on the plans that were never built. The Tower Block was built - strangely enough it was built 64 flats to 64 shops, with the naive thought that there would be 64 managers managing the 64 units in the centre and living in the flats upstairs. That never happened – the flats were never luxury flats as they*

Trees being uprooted during the clearance works for the Tower Centre

were meant to be – they were quite basic and were criticised for being very basic at the time." Brian Walsh of Meadows was another trader who was disconcerted by what he saw going up. *"We didn't know what to think about it initially and it was only when it went up and up and up we suddenly realised – 'hang on a minute, not sure if we like this.' But by that time it was too late – it was there. My opinion - and I still feel that - it's just far too high for the High Street. Such a shame."*

Malcolm and his father were desperate to move into their new premises in order to get their business back up and running and so they were allowed early admittance to the precinct, which had its drawbacks. *"Because it wasn't finished we couldn't gain access to our front door, so we traded for nearly 12 months from our back entrance. I can remember distinctly one time when we were eventually allowed to go out of our front door. One evening in the dark I walked out across the centre which wasn't finished and stepped on to what I thought was a black large paved area as I was walking across to the Clock Tower - only to find that I fell down a hole! I managed to cling on to the other side of the hole otherwise I could have fallen down into the basement, into the car park as it was then."*

View over the construction site from the roof of Tower Heights (1966)

Grand Opening

In May 1967 a bright, shining, modern concrete edifice called the Tower Centre was officially opened with great ceremony, but very little public enthusiasm. Having bought out the *Hoddesdon Journal* and promptly discontinued it, the *Mercury* was left to cover the event. Henry Ronson, Chairman of the Heron Group, told the paper: *"Older traders in the town are living in the past and cannot offer the younger generation what they want. In future shoppers will move to the precinct end of the town and the old established shops at the opposite end will die. But this is progress, and things move on, and it has got to happen everywhere. History must move over and make way for the modern age."*

Whilst many younger people in the town greeted their new facility with initial enthusiasm, disillusionment set in pretty quickly. Annette Marples was one of them.*" I think we all thought it was going to be this wonderful shopping centre, but there were good shops down there - there was Dorothy Perkins down there; and a Boots; the bowling alley, of course. But as I say, I think a lot of people were disappointed when they built that awful tower block. I know people have got to be housed, but I think it was more than what people thought it was going to be."*

"At the time, being a teenager, we thought it was a good thing", say Les Riches, *"best thing that had ever happened to Hoddesdon... Because we always used to say 'You can't get anything in Hoddesdon – it's not very good for shopping. Ah, when they do this Tower Centre it will be wonderful.' Of course it was the biggest white elephant ever."* William Smith had a similar reaction. *"The 1960s were a refreshing time, the Coronation had happened and we'd lived in very austere times before the early 60's. Things were going forward, I suppose... It was quite an innovation because it was a high-rise structure, totally out of place in Hoddesdon at the time. No, I was quite disgusted by that, but obviously one can't live in the past."*

A White Elephant

But right from the start problems emerged with the basic design - the block of flats above was funnelling the wind down into the precinct below. The manager of one of the new shops described the consequences as: *"Not so much a wind - more a hurricane! All the time we get complaints from customers about draughts. But apart from that I think it is fine here."* In the second edition of the Hertfordshire volume of his series '*Buildings of England*' the architectural historian Nikolaus Pevsner

The new Tower Centre Precinct (1967)

was scathing. *"An ugly nine storey block of flats in drab grey concrete standing on stilts above a shopping precinct… It is undoubtedly the most unappealing example in the country of the 1960s craze for re-modelling town centres"* Tim Turner remembers, *"I met a chap once who worked as a town planner and said that when he was at college they were brought to visit the Tower Centre to show how **not** to design town centres!"*

The greatest success of the whole development was the inclusion of a bowling alley, as young mum Annette Marples remembers. *"The bowling alley was right down in the corner, where Argos was, and it used to be quite a good night out. My children used to like going up there as well. But also it kept the children off the streets - at least they were there, you knew they were reasonably safe in there."* Sadly, as George Don explains, this popular venue did not last. *"My wife was pleased because there was a bowling alley and she was a member of a women's team that used the bowling alley. Everyone was beginning to accept it as it was – think it was great. But after the fire at the bowling alley it all started to deteriorate."*

Brian Walsh admits that initially he was concerned about the impact on their store when they heard a Tesco outlet was opening in the new precinct. *"But it wasn't terribly successful, I believe, and it didn't affect us to any great degree. I don't think the Tower Centre had that much impact on the rest of the town to be perfectly honest – it was never a howling success down there. And I believe it was never fully occupied, the shops, at any time – there were always empty units, one way or another. And you know the Tesco there - the bowling alley fire, very convenient, took out the Tesco as well. And ironically they are now back in our old building – a strange twist."*

Local historian and former Librarian, Edward Paddick, was much less forgiving. *"No one but the developers would appear to be any better off for the coming of the Tower Shopping Centre, within a short time of it opening many of the shop keepers had to apply for a reduction of rates, and their position will have probably become worse since the opening of the Fawkon Walk Shopping Centre… I suggest had there been a Master Plan for the town the eventual development of the shopping centre at Fawkon Walk could have been extended and planned to hold all the additional shops that it was felt the town needed, obviating the necessity for the erection of the monstrous Tower Centre."* In 2014 the campaign against the building of High Leigh 'Garden Village' has been hampered by the fact that Broxbourne District Council has failed to produce the Local Plan required of them by the Government.

In the mid 1980s the ugly, draughty and unpopular shopping centre underwent a major re-vamp and then changed ownership several times, but this didn't stem the gradual trickle of retailers relocating elsewhere.

During the 1990s former childhood star Lena Zavaroni moved into Tower Heights. She'd been just nine years old when she'd won the TV talent show 'Opportunity Knocks' and been catapulted to instant stardom. But the pressure of such early fame had led her to develop anorexia nervosa at 13. Her career had fizzled out by the time she reached her early 20s and she moved to Hoddesdon after splitting from her husband in 1991, where she lived on income support of less than £50 per week. She befriended several local people over the next decade, including singer Ray Dexter. She died at the tragically young age of 35 in January 2000 in the aftermath of a risky operation to cure her anorexia weighing just four stone.

Despite a final makeover costing £6m in 2008, over two thirds of the retail units in the Tower Centre remained empty. Then, to everyone's amazement, the precinct was suddenly sold to a property development company in 2011 who subsequently secured a commission to build a new Morrisons supermarket on the site. In a major construction programme lasting over 18 months *(see page 117)* the whole rear section of the complex was demolished to make way for a large retail unit with a car park below and additional parking at ground level out the front. The new Morrisons supermarket opened on schedule in the first week of December 2013.

But Malcolm Norris deserves to have the final say in this sad and sorry saga. *"With hindsight I wish we'd moved away and my father had invested the money in another property, but that's with hindsight. That's what I wanted at the time... All of the shops came into the Tower Centre and every single one was a large multiple – we had Tesco, we had Woolworths, we had Dorothy Perkins, we had Boots, on and on and on. At Norris we were the only little independent shop and they told us at the time: 'Yes, you can come into the Tower Centre, you can have a unit but you will never survive in the climate of the big shops.' And the irony is, that we did - and all the big shops left by the time we packed up the shop in the Tower Centre finally in 2001."*

ST KATHERINE'S CHAPEL

We now turn our attention to the area immediately in front of the Tower Centre complex which was once the site of the town's original and most ancient place of worship, St Katherine's Chapel. It first gets mentioned in a record of the Court of the King's Bench in 1242. In 1336 William de la Marche – the king's cook – obtained a grant of *"a certain vacant space at Hoddesdon, so that he may build anew on the aforesaid space a chapel in honour of St Catherine and that he may give that chapel to any chaplain or man of religion that he may choose."*

It was probably a timbered and plaster building with an open gable housing two bells, clearly intended to cater for pilgrims en route to the famous shrine at Walsingham. It also became a focus for civic life according to Tregelles: *"A wife's settlement was executed in the porch, purchase-monies for estates were to be paid in the chapel, mortgages were discharged therein, proclamation of strays by the bailiff was ordered to be made there, and everything goes to prove that it was used as the public exchange."*

By 1651 the chapel was in a poor state having lost its endowments and with insufficient income for its upkeep. By 1700 it was closed and in a ruinous condition, but at a vestry meeting at Broxbourne Church in October it was *"agreed by the inhabitants of Hoddesdon that ye*

18th century print of the Clock House

churchwardens do sell one of yr bells in Hoddesdon chapel to by a new clock for ye said chapel." This led to an anonymous ditty being coined:

*Parson Davis and Farmer Lock
Sold their bell to buy a clock.*

A new clock house containing a room for a resident bellringer was completed in 1705 and the new clock manufactured by John Fordham of Dunmow Magna was subsequently installed. In 1719 Parish records report that Jonathan Ward *"is appointed to live in the clock house to ring the bell at 4 o clock in the morning and 8 o clock in the evening."*

The *'Every-day Book and Table Book: Or Everlasting Calendar of Popular Amusements'*, written in 1826 by William Hones, tells us that the old curfew bell *"at Hoddesdon in Hertfordshire which was anciently rung in that town for the extinction and relighting of 'allfire and candlelight' still exists, and has from time immemorial been rung on the morning of Shrove Tuesday at 4 o clock, after which hour the inhabitants were at liberty to make and eat pancakes until the bell rings again at 8 o clock at night. This custom is said to be so closely observed that after that hour not a pancake remains in the town."*

THE CLOCK TOWER

In 1835 the decrepit Clock House was demolished and a new Clock Tower was erected, funded by public subscription and donations from wealthy local residents. It had a number of small rooms at its base used for vestry meetings and gatherings of local societies as well as housing the town's fire engine, and so became known as the 'Town Hall'. One room was rented by the Chief Constable of Hertfordshire to serve as the HQ of the town police force which consisted of a sergeant and one constable.

In 1857 one of Hoddesdon's constables, PC Mingay, had made himself hugely unpopular to the point that handbills were produced by local printer Robert Rippon on behalf of the residents complaining of his high-handedness and calling for his dismissal with a poem entitled *'Tyranny in the 19th Century'*.

*In a neat little town, four miles south of Ware,
There is stationed a Peeler so fast and severe,
That he's stirring up strife, and ruining trade,
While many hard things of the poor he has said.*

He makes us out thieves and says we should tremble,
And if two or three in the street do assemble,
He comes, and he crawls around them, and spies,
His ear to their converse he quickly applies.

Things here have arisen to such a high pitch,
That it seems like the French reign of terror;
But surely before many months have gone by,
Old Bloaters will find out his error.

In June of that same year Ware magistrates dismissed charges brought by PC Mingay against several locals supposedly involved in a disturbance at the Bell Inn at Hoddesdon. This blow to his authority seems to have resulted in him subsequently being transferred elsewhere - no doubt with cries of 'good riddance' ringing in his ears!

According to Tregelles *"In 1869 the clock (169 years old) was reported to be much worn, and it was decided to raise subscriptions for the purchase of a new clock from Gillet & Bland of Croydon. In 1871 the new clock with its illuminated dials was in position, the amount spent being reported as £151 3s. 8d."* In the late 1890s the building is still listed as the 'Town Hall', with George Smith working there as its Keeper.

Miss Ashford's Kindergarten School at the Clock Tower. Mollie Muetzel is third from left in middle row (late 1920s)

In the early years just prior to the First World War it served as the terminus for Hoddedon's first omnibus, as described by Paddick. *"It was owned and driven by Sam Pigott, and was drawn by one hard working horse; it was black in colour and had a narrow board running along each side showing its destination... and route. Passengers entered through a door at the rear by means of a step set below the door, and sat facing the centre on seats fixed below the small windows, which let a pale light into the bus. The driver sat on the box, almost on top of the bus, and the foot board of the box stretched out above the horse's flanks. It had four wheels, two small ones at the front and two larger ones at the rear."*

By the 1920s a nursery was being run in one of the rooms with young Mollie Muetzel in attendance. *"We didn't go to school until we were five in those days... My sister was there first, five years before me, and it was Miss Ashford's Kindergarten School.... We had Wednesdays off because it was market day, we couldn't have heard ourselves speak... But Miss Ashford was absolutely fantastic. This photo (page 103) shows a play we did at school, like they do now I suppose."*

Proclamation of Elizabeth II on 6th February 1952

From the late 19th century onwards the Clock Tower was the focus of important events to celebrate various national occasions such as royal weddings, jubilees and proclamations.

The Clock Tower was also where the Carnival Queen was crowned when Hoddesdon's first post-war carnival was held to celebrate the Festival of Britain in 1951. *'Thousands Enjoy Carnival'*, was the headline in the *Journal*. *"From early in the morning there was an atmosphere of expectancy and excitement, which increased as flags and bunting appeared, and decorated vehicles began to wend their way towards the procession meeting place... After thanking the crowd for their reception, the Carnival Queen, Miss Pamela O'Neill, called the people in the following words to keep Carnival:*

> *People of Hoddesdon, let us be gay*
> *On this, our festival carnival day.*
> *Put aside your cares and labours*
> *And join the fun with friends and neighbours.*
> *Let us rejoice in Britain's name*
> *And for today let carnival reign."*

However, it wasn't until 1966 that a Town Carnival was established on an annual basis every September – which then ran for the next 40 years. Richard Thomas served for many years on the Carnival Committee. "*I*

Carnival procession (1930s)

came to live in Hoddesdon in 1967 and got involved with the carnival the following year when we built a float for Admirals Walk... We eventually settled in 1971 on using the 100 Acre Estate which was perfect – a mile long road, and the ability to form the carnival up in a fairly limited space."

The procession made its way down Stanstead Road, through the High Street and then on southwards to end with a fete at Deaconsfield in Broxbourne. In the 1970s virtually every local organization and business in the town was participating in a colourful and lively spectacle which included celebrity names of the time like actresses Diana Dors and Pat Phoenix from Coronation Street, Formula One racing driver James Hunt, and even the famous race horse, Red Rum.

Above: *Carnival Parade (1966)*

'*The Clock Tower - Next for Demolition?*' asked a horrified reporter in the *Hoddesdon Journal* in January 1965, "*Some people think the Clock Tower will look dilapidated and out of place alongside the new buildings that are springing up around it.*" This time HUDC carried out a public consultation and, although the rooms below were subsequently demolished, the iconic tower itself survived, albeit looking rather ungainly shorn of its base. The addition of a canopy paid for by the Hoddesdon Society some years later was a considerable aesthetic improvement.

The Clock Tower was even the scene of a re-enactment of the crucifixion of Christ on Good Friday 1979 when a large-scale Passion Play was performed in the town. Rev P J Gandon, the vicar of the Parish Church, brought together churches from all over the area to help stage this ambitious project. The different episodes that made up the Passion story were performed on makeshift stages around the town with the Last Supper inside the Tower Centre and the Trial of Christ taking place in Fawkon Walk outside Sainsbury's.

John Allison, one of the main performers, explains that the next stage "*was the carrying of the cross through town to the High Street to the Clock Tower where the staging of the crucifixion was held. I, for my sins, as one of the two thieves on the cross beside Jesus, and my friend Simon Sheldon was the other thief on the other side. I was on the right, and he was on the left. It was quite imposing; the cross must have been about 12 to 15 feet off the ground on staging. And it was just quite a stunning experience with hundreds of people around, and the effect it had on the local population. It did make a very worthwhile and memorable Easter for us.*"

THE BELL INN (1, Burford Street) currently still in situ

We now need to walk just a couple of hundred yards across the road to look at the buildings on the East side of the street. Leading away to our left is Burford Street which, up until the mid 19th century, was known as Stanstead Valley. Here we find the last remaining historic inn to survive in the town, the Bell. It appears to have been built as a private house in the 16th century and is first mentioned in records in 1546, owned by John Conysby, Rector of the Parish of Great Amwell. It became the Holly Bush Inn, then the Blue Bell, before finally getting its current name in the 1660s, possibly due to its proximity to St Katherine's Chapel which contained the bell paid for by Sir William Say in 1511.

Bell Lane, running down the north side of the property, originally led to the common meads and was known as 'Jordan's Lane', later 'Alderwyk' or 'Aldwyk' Lane. Once it continued further west across the main highway and linked up with Paul's Lane over by the church. In 1835 the Bell was bought by the owners of Hoddesdon Brewery and in the late 1890s George Cleeve was the publican. Early in the twentieth century landlord T Child was aiming to attract a new clientele by offering food and accommodation for the many enthusiastic Edwardian cyclists who were thronging the highways and byways at this time.

THE PAVILION CINEMA (136, High Street) currently Tollgate Brokers and Mieszko Delicatessen

We're looking now at the site of the Four Feathers Inn mentioned in 1663 that was later incorporated into the brewery complex. With the sudden and unexpected closure of the brewery in the late 1930s *(see page 125)* this portion was sold off and re-developed as the Pavilion Cinema in 1930.

The Pavilion Cinema (1930s)

Young Tommy Knight was in attendance. *"I actually went to the opening of it; I must have been about nine. I think my mother was supposed to go but she wasn't well and an Aunt took me."* Diana Borchards has fond memories of the full sized Christie organ which was installed in 1933. *"It cost 3d downstairs but the balcony was 6d - a big treat... before the show started a man playing an organ was lifted up on a platform in front of the curtain, and lowered again once the film began."*

Saturday morning pictures were a great treat for generations of Hoddesdon kids like Les Riches. *"You walked in, the box office was in front of you, then there were two corridors – one to the stalls and one to the balcony on the right hand side. You got your main film and then you got a supporting act, between that you got the ads – Shipman and King's stuff. Saturday morning you got all the cowboy films, Batman and Robin - that sort of thing."*

Although the Government closed all cinemas when war broke out in 1939, they quickly re-opened when it was realised how incredibly important they were in maintaining civilian morale, as Mary Newton recalls: *"They put a notice up on the screen at the cinema, to say that the air raid sirens had sounded, if you wanted to leave. I can't remember anyone ever leaving; they just used to carry on with it. That was quite interesting going to the cinema then, because there was no heating so we all used to troop along with blankets. But we used to see such a lot of the lovely old American musicals, which cheered everyone up."*

The Pavilion Cinema's magnificent Christie organ (1930s)

As Joan Umney reminds us, a trip to the 'flicks' still meant personal service as late as the 1950s. *"The doorman that used to see you going in was always in a proper uniform – I think that was a plum sort of colour."* *"You were received by the usherette,"* says Arthur Wingate, *"and she had a torch, which she shone down on the ground, because the edges of the steps were all painted white, and she would show you to your seats."*

And you got real value for money, Peter Shepherd remembers. *"In those days, you would have had a small film probably lasting three quarters of an hour or so, usually followed then by the interval when the organ came up and was played. And then the feature film, whatever it might have been, followed that. Ice creams would have been served in the interval, and the adverts probably to start with. A newsreel - Pathe or British Gaumont News - which would be usually in the middle."*

Ironically the cinema itself became the star in a British film in August 1963, when part of '*Night Must Fall*' was made in the area. Two of the stars, Susan Hampshire and Sheila Hancock, appeared in several scenes shot in the High Street. The *Journal*'s reporter was there. *"These were two interesting days in which Hoddesdon's Clock Tower and High Street became the focal point of interest, activity and conversation. Particularly on the first day when filming continued for some 12 hours. To add rain swept realism to the scenes being shot, hoses played relentlessly on the Market Square under direction of the men of the Hertfordshire Fire Brigade. Floodlights placed at several points added a somewhat macabre glint to the scene which was watched by over 1000 people."*

Hedley Eariss was one of those avid spectators. *"That featured what was then quite a sensational car: a Mini convertible that came down the High Street, pulled into a parking bay and the lady got out and walked away. That was all the scene was that was shot there. But we stood watching it one whole day. I don't know how many times they did it - it seemed like forever. It went on for hours and hours - for what in the film, I believe, was about a two-minute shot."*

By the late 1960s film audiences were in what appeared to be terminal decline, and the Pavilion was sold off and re-opened as a Bingo Hall in 1972. In 1987 it was a Zetters Leisure & Social Club; they were succeeded by Coral who gave the frontage a garish makeover. *(see page 115)* It was eventually demolished just before the millennium to make way for a bland block containing two small retail units with flats above.

111

Clock Tower and War Memorial (late 1920s/early1930s)

Bull Hotel and west side of High Street (c1900s)

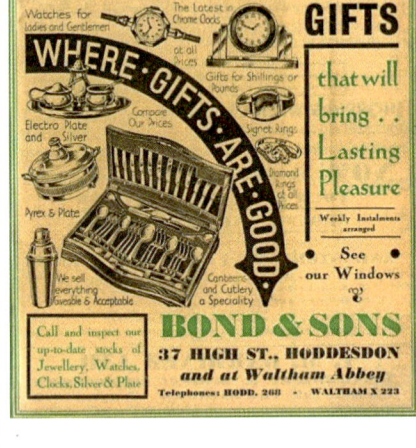

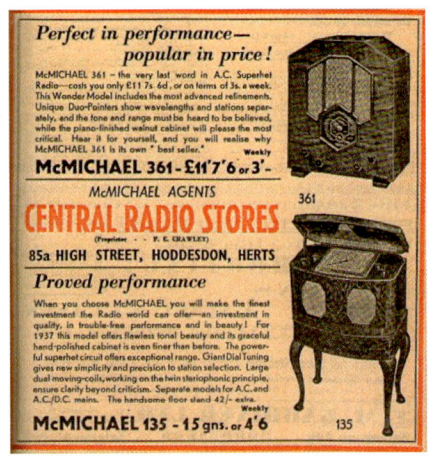

Hoddesdon Journal Adverts 1930s – 1950s.

Receipts and statements from Hoddesdon businesses (1930s)

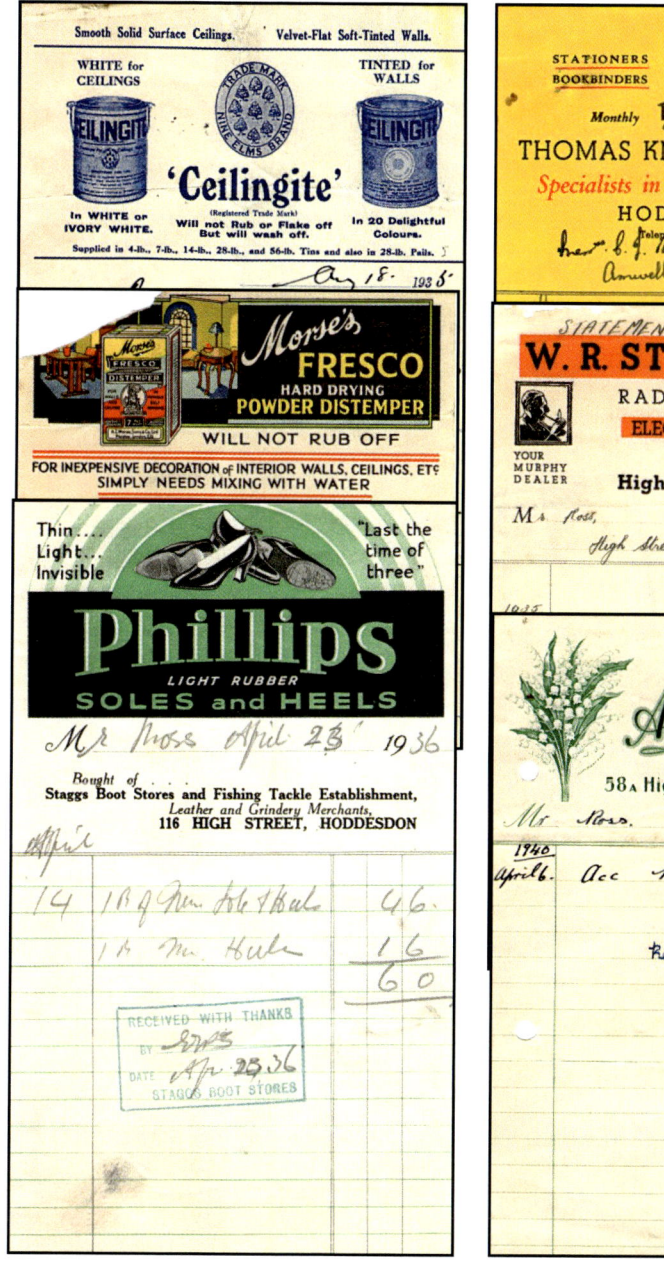

Architect's impression of Tower Centre (1965)

High Street including Tower Centre and Clock Tower (c1970)

115

Hoddesdon High Street (1980s – 90s)

Top to bottom: *Fawkon Walk (late 1980s); Fawkon Walk re-development (2008); Yet another Tower Centre re-vamp (2008)*

Construction of new Morrisons Supermarket (2012-13)

Top to Bottom: *Classic Car Rally (2006); Charter Fair (2010); the Woodlands Orangery (2005)*

FORDHAM & CO (134, High Street) currently the Trading Centre

This long-established Hoddesdon store opened in October 1934 in a building leased from the Rochford family – the owner, W S Fordham, already had branches operating in Puckeridge and had opened a Hertford shop in 1921. His son William (known as Bill) took over the business and ran it until his death in 1956 when his brother Douglas gave up his job in banking to run the family firm. At this stage the company had opened a pram and children's toyshop almost opposite on the west side of Hoddesdon High Street, and by the early 1970s were running a bed shop on the corner of Brewery Road managed by Sheila Williams.

Douglas Fordham's daughter married Bernard Marshall and their son Keith started working in Hertford as a teenager in the early 1970s. He was sent to help out in the Hoddesdon branch on a number of occasions. Both shops were run by Douglas, who Keith remembers as *"a very neat man, always immaculately dressed, short and rather rotund."* Manager Stanley Williams had worked at the shop right from the day it opened.

Fordham's Furniture Store (late 1950s)

Brian Thurston worked full time in the shop, alongside part time sales staff Keith Bright and Arthur Dent. Another long-serving member of staff was Betty Brace who started with the company aged 14 and worked until her retirement at 64. *"John Bracey was our delivery driver, working exclusively for us unlike today when most deliveries are done by contract staff... he followed on from his father who had worked for us doing the same job,"* Keith remembers. The teenager was very impressed by the fact that the staff in Hoddesdon enjoyed free cheese and crackers during their morning breaks, something that didn't happen back at Hertford. He also regularly got bought ice creams by Sheila Williams.

Keith describes the shop: " *You came in the main entrance which was the furniture department, and there was a large staircase right in front of you which went up to a mezzanine where we had small furniture items like pouffes... on the first floor were dining tables and the carpet department was up there.* " The basement contained the upholstery department, while on the second floor there was a store room. Of course there were no lifts, with the building having once been part of the old brewery complex, and Keith recalls *"we often had to lug bits of furniture up there via the outside fire escape... Out the back of the shop was a yard used for staff parking and there were two corrugated iron sheds used to store carpets and furniture."*

George Don went to the local furniture store when he and his wife set up home. *"When I got married and came back to live in Hoddesdon in 1963 you went in and there was furniture on the left and the right and then in front of you there was an enormous staircase – very wide and there*

Company founder William Fordham (left) and Douglas Fordham (right)

By the late 1990s this was the first home of Panache children's wear, which later moved down to a unit in Fawkon Walk, before ending up in its current location on the west side of the High Street at number 55A.

THE HODDESDON BREWERY

If we now cross the top of Brewery Road to the south side and turn to look back we see that the last few shops we've just been viewing are housed in monolithic blocks which were once part of Hoddesdon's brewery.

A brewery owned by Robert Plomer is documented as early as 1736. Around the same time as starting a bank in Hertford in 1805, William Christie from Fife in Scotland and George Cathrow purchased the brewery from the Whittingstall family who had been owners since 1781. Rev Jones of Broxbourne records in his diary a visit from one of the new owners. *"Mr Christie did me the favour of a call and very liberally presented me with a £10 note of his and Mr Cathrow's bank, in my estimation of equal value at least with a Bank of England note... Mr Christie further gratified me by a very acceptable present and his very delicate and respectful manner of conferring it increases its value a hundred fold. It was no less than a gown, cassock, and the whole paraphernalia of a parson."*

On the death of Mr Cathrow in 1840 a strange custom was started as specified in his will, according to the Timbs book previously mentioned

The Christie Brewery (c1900)

was more stuff on the next floor. We used to buy all sorts of furniture in there and carpets. And he used to run a book - a small card - where you could pay a shilling a week, sixpence a week, or whatever you wanted. You went in there and paid what you could and the manager ticked it off – there was never any bother."

When Douglas retired, Keith purchased the Hertford shop from the family in 1985, changing its name to Marshalls which is what is still operates as today. Three years after celebrating half a century of trading in the town, the Hoddesdon shop closed in 1987 and became a sports retailer called Race Rags.

SUITALL VALET SERVICE LTD (132 + 132A, High Street) currently Jet Dry Cleaners and Changes Hair Salon

From the 1930s until the late 1940s this modest shop housed a dry cleaning and clothes repair business called the Suitall Valet Service which also had branches in Ware and Hertford. The company had a prime advertising spot on the first page of the Hoddesdon Journal for nearly a decade. A 1935 advert read: *'Brains Get the Job but Appearance Gets the Interview: Dry Cleaning is the cheapest form of appearance insurance. Any coat, suit or costume perfectly cleaned and pressed for 3/6d.'*

By the mid 1950s this had become a branch of Dane Cleaners and Dyers, who had a dozen other outlets in Herts & Essex. Mary Young worked for them in the 1950s. *"The shop was over by the clock and the works were in Brocket Road. I worked in the ironing room – we had all the presses – our room had one press, the rest was all ironing. And we had the wet room where things were washed – there were some dirty people about I'm afraid."*

Even today, in an unusual example of continuity, there is still a dry cleaners operating in the same premises. In the right hand side of the building in 1963 Michele was running her hairdressing salon, and the same service also continues to be offered there today.

CORNER HOUSE (130, High Street) currently Hoddesdon Cafe

For over 30 years from the mid 1930s this property was known as the 'Corner House' – a tobacconist that also sold children's books, party games, greetings cards, calendars and *'Fancy Boxes of Chocolates by the Best Makers'*. *"You very rarely went into the shop itself,"* says Mary Young, *"because if you went into Brewery Road there was a window there and that's where you could go and get your ice cream."*

'Something for Everybody'. *"A barrel of beer, which was always to be kept full, fixed in a stand in the High Street opposite the Brewery, with an iron pot chained to a post for every passer-by to drink. For some time after the owner's decease it was a cask of good ale, then it was reduced to table beer, and finally abolished."* This was obviously much to the satisfaction of the landlords of the Maidenhead and Bell Inns, who had lodged complaints about the damage this bequest was doing to their trade.

In 1842 a consortium, which included Charles Peter Christie, bought the brewery – they had the whole complex re-built, as well as purchasing several local public houses. Mr Christie, educated at Eton and married to Isabel Perkins of Lord Street, became the sole owner in 1865. Hayllar describes him as, *"a man of strong will, unflagging perseverance, and sound common sense, so that in whatever sphere he moved he was always highly respected, his opinions always carrying great weight."* Mr Christie was very proud of his stable of fine horses which were used to pull the brewery carts and drays which delivered the beer around the area. He stipulated that the cart driver had to walk on foot at his horse's head for a mile before he entered any town and for the same distance on his way out.

The success of the business was partly attributed to the use of fresh water supplied from its own well on the premises. The complex also included a covered public swimming pool accessed via Bell Lane - which was heated as a by-product of the brewing process. The pool became the home of the

C P Christie being driven along the High Street (c1890s)

Hoddesdon Swimming Club and was enormously popular with locals, including William Smith's father. *"Mr Harry Stag owned the shoe shop... he and my father were great friends and used to as children, or young men, swim in the swimming pool... I actually have some certificates of my father winning several races there - it was kind of a bit of a competition between Harry Stag and my father because, apparently, they were some of the best swimmers there at the time."*

In winter the pool was boarded over and used as a venue for concerts and other public performances. Mary Newton remembers her mother talking about attending plays there in 1920s, many of which included musical interludes.

When C P Christie died in 1898 his four sons took over running the business until a private company was formed in 1903, by which time it owned 124 inns and beerhouses across the county - out of the 24 in Hoddesdon itself, 16 belonged to the brewery. There was a major fire on the night of 3rd Jan 1905 - the 34 horses in the stables were put in considerable danger during the blaze, and were only just rescued in time by staff. Two maltings and a number of ancillary buildings were destroyed at an estimated cost of more than £10,000. Hardly surprising that Tommy Knight's earliest memory of Hoddesdon *"goes back to when I was small enough to be sat on the shoulders of my uncle and watching the new fire engine tested by squirting water right up the front of the brewery. And, of course, in those days it was a steam engine."*

Demolition of the brewery (c1930)

After the First World War the fortunes of the brewery were in decline - Hayllar describes what happened next. *"It was felt to be a real blow in many ways when, as from the end of March 1928 the business was absorbed into a larger concern, the Cannon Brewery Co, later to come under the control of Taylor, Walker & Co. Much of the building was then pulled down, including the tall chimney on the main block, which had been quite a landmark."*

Whilst some of the remaining buildings were sold off for alternative business uses, the effect on the economy of the town just at the start of the 1930s must have been quite severe, with many local people suddenly finding themselves out of work at the start of the greatest economic slump the modern world had ever experienced.

BREWERY ROAD

If we walk just a few hundred yards down Brewery Road we can still see the remains of parts of various old brewery premises which today have been converted into a mixture shops, houses, flats, a nightclub and various industrial units. In 1930 it was somewhere down here that Tommy Knight's father Thomas bought the old bottling plant to house his successful printing business which had outgrown its premises in the High Street. *(see page 143)*

"He bought various bits of property in Brewery Road as the years went by," Tommy explains, *"and expanded the business that was known as Thomas Knight: The Clockhouse Press. And in 1950 he also bought up a carton-making business and brought it down to Hoddesdon in a new building on the opposite side of Brewery Road. And that flourished very well, and at the peak we had about 150 staff altogether."*

April 1935 saw the launch of what was to become one of the town's most fondly-remembered local publications. Tommy describes its genesis. *"In the mid 1930's we printed the Worthing Journal and my father took up the idea to start a Hoddesdon Journal. First of all a local footballer who also worked for us a compositor - Charlie Martin - became the editor and he built up interest in the town. 'Onlooker' was Charlie - he never actually had a by-line, but he always went under that name. Lots of people never actually knew when he was around, and so they had to be careful not to let out any secrets."*

In the first edition of the *Hoddesdon Journal*, 'Onlooker' introduced himself and the paper. *"People of Hoddesdon and district – How Do You Do? I am most happy to have made your acquaintance. In this town of*

Tommy Knight (2nd from left) with 'Onlooker' Charlie Martin (4th from left) and other former Thomas Knight staff (1986)

progressive-minded people my arrival seems most opportune and growth in the near future is a certainty. Now, about myself. I am all-Hoddesdon. I am produced in Hoddesdon by Hoddesdon labour, edited locally, and the "text" is the functioning of a first-quality Hoddesdon brain."

For the first six years the enormously popular publication appeared in a magazine format measuring 24cm x 18cm, and was delivered free to all homes in the district each month. It was crammed with local advertising, film listings and personal ads alongside news snippets, reports of council meetings, profiles of local personalities and businesses, as well as a sports section with match results. But the paper suddenly ceased publication in July 1941 when the supply of newsprint became the latest product to be rationed. But Tommy's enterprising father came up with a plan to get his *Journal* back in print the following year. *"During the war, in order to get paper allocated, we had to be registered as a newspaper so we changed the format and became a small broadsheet, and it built up from there."*

When Tommy came back in to the firm after being de-mobbed, his father asked him to take over the running of the *Journal*. His editorial line for the next two decades was very straightforward. *"I used to look out for local things. In fact, that was it really - we were a local paper, we didn't try and pretend to be a national paper and have all the nasty bits in as well as the local news."*

The paper's many readers must have been shocked to read on the front page of the March1967 edition that the *Journal* title had been sold to their local rival the *Mercury*. Hardly surprisingly, the *Hoddesdon Journal*'s name soon disappeared from the amalgamated paper's masthead. In 1980 Tommy and his brother closed their family business and the various components of the site were sold off. By this time the Hoddesdon Business Centre had appeared down the end of the road, which included a factory where the massively popular 'Workmate' was manufactured. *(see page 32)*

BREWERY HOUSE

C.P Christie originally lived in this house next to the entrance to his Brewery which still features a charming stone carving of two 'putti' or cherubs harvesting hops. Mr Christie later moved down to his grand new mansion at the south end of town *(see page 166)* and this building became the Brewery Offices. It would appear that part of the north end of the building was knocked down, presumably in 1930, to widen the entrance to the new Brewery Road.

Brewery House (late C19th)

This property is rumoured to have been constructed on the site of the Thatched House Inn mentioned in Izaak Walton's '*The Compleat Angler.*' Tregelles writes: *"We have no earlier name for this, and doubtless the title was originally used to distinguish it from the tiled buildings of the town. It probably became an Inn about 1600, and is described in the vestry book of 1737 as 'Mr Plomer's Brewhouse'"*.

ROBERTS'S HOTEL AND CAFÉ (128A, High Street) currently IPR Recruitment

If we peep round the northern side of the building flanking Brewery Road we'd have found the entrance to Roberts's Café. In 1935 it would have cost a traveller just four shillings (20p) for bed and breakfast here. You could get food served in the café from breakfast to supper. Mary Young knew the owners. *"We used to go there for meals. I think it was a café downstairs, but we used to go upstairs for home cooked meals."* Around the front of the premises the ground floor housed three shops.

ABBOTT TAILORS (128, High Street) currently Shake 'n' Smooth

Abbott High Grade Tailoring was offering menswear services here by the mid 1930s – the owner advertising himself as a tailor *'trained by Herbert*

Shops and restaurant (1963)

Chappell Ltd of Gresham Street, London EC'. In 1935 you could get a made to measure suit from 50 shillings (£2.50)

DEWHURST BUTCHERS (126, High Street) currently iSmashedit

A local butcher traded here up until the post war period when a branch of the Dewhurst chain came to town.

F CLEMENT GROCER (124, High Street) currently KFC takeaway

Another privately owned grocery store, which in the mid 1930s boasted that it was *'Noted for Finest Bacon and Cooked Hams in the District,'* continued to serve local customers until well into the 1960s.

In June 2006 a serious fire broke out on the first floor of this historic block and caused considerable damage, although thankfully no one was injured and the plaster panel escaped with minor blackening. However, 128 Cafe, Zax Boutique and the Marie Curie Charity shop on the ground floor remained closed for over 18 months. The cafe was modernised and extended to the first floor and opened under the new name of Brewery Bites, while Zax resumed trading for several more years before throwing in the towel. However, the Marie Curie store was replaced by a Kentucky Fried Chicken outlet, in spite of Broxbourne Council's stated policy of prohibiting any more takeaway restaurants from opening in the town centre.

QUEEN VICTORIA'S DIAMOND JUBILEE

If we now execute a 180 degree turn to look behind us, just over 100 years ago our view would have been completely blocked by an enormous 210 ft long marquee. This had been erected to accommodate a feast for the 'deserving poor of the parish' as part of the celebration of the Diamond Jubilee of Queen Victoria in 1897. We have a wonderful series of contemporary photographs *(see page 130)* showing the High Street bedecked with bunting, and thronged with townsfolk of all classes out in their Sunday best, listening to speeches from local dignitaries before moving off to Lowfield for a special fete. The highlight of the evening's entertainments was an illuminated cycle procession.

HODDESDON MARKET

This area spread out in front of us at the widest part of the High Street was the site of the Market Place for centuries. There has been a weekly market in Hoddesdon since Henry III gave a royal grant for a Thursday market

Queen Victoria's Diamond Jubilee featuring a giant marquee (1897)

back in 1253 when Richard de Boxe was given the right "*to hold a market at his aforesaid manor of Hoddesdon on Thursday of each week and that forever there may be a fair once a year lasting for three days: on the eve, the day, and the morrow of St Martin.*" This was 10th – 12th November. In 1469 Sir John Say obtained a re-grant of the market privileges from Edward IV, thereby effectively curtailing an earlier grant to Hertford by Henry VI for a weekly market to the exclusion of any other within a seven mile radius, "*greatly to the annoyance of Hertford, whose bailiffs repeatedly tried for the next 100 years to stop the holding of a market in Hoddesdon,*" Tregelles reports.

Originally there was a market cross on this site – first mentioned in 1256, probably in the form of a plain oak cross. This was superseded by a more elaborate structure which was hexagonal on a brick foundation. According to Tregelles: "*The market grew with the increase of traffic and before the end of the sixteenth century was famous for its malt... Butchers' and fishmongers' stalls were permanent buildings, and besides these were the numerous 'pitched' stalls, some evidently pens set in the ground and subject to a distinct toll known as 'piccage'. Even the chapel-side and end were used by lean-to stalls and shops.*"

At some point in the Middle Ages the stalls in this part of the High Street became permanent structures and developed into 'middle row' – as happened in many market towns. Middle Row in Hoddesdon survived until the middle of the 19th century and features in a photo of 1851 showing the aftermath of the annual fair. But, along with many similar features of towns all over the country, they were deemed to be impeding the increasing flow of road traffic and were demolished in 1857 by C P Christie.

However, by 1670 the Herts Session Rolls report: *"that the market cross of Hodsdon is so much out of repayre that the market people cannot sit under it as formerly they did without danger of their lives and that the people of Hoddesdon ought to repair the same."* In the end it was the coming of the railways that finished off the market, which had probably ceased to exist by the mid 19th century.

In 1886 Mr Bridgman, an auctioneer, set up a cattle market on Wednesdays a little to the south of market place stretching from outside Gardiners and down to the corner of Conduit Lane. Edward Paddick's book contains a charming description of what market day was like in his childhood. *"On Wednesday mornings we would meet, on our way to school, herds of sheep and droves of bullocks, and sometimes pigs, being driven on the hoof to Hoddesdon market... There was always a chance of some excitement on market day, usually caused by cattle being confined for long periods breaking away and dashing down any side street. I do not remember anyone being seriously hurt on these occasions, but damage was often done to fences and gardens in the process of getting them under control."*

After the 1914-18 war stalls began to appear round the Clock Tower selling general goods – and in the early 1920s local traders complained to Hoddesdon UDC that they should be regulated, with local businesses allowed to compete by operating their own stalls. This was agreed, but proved to be unprofitable and so, in the end, the market continued to largely consist of outsiders. The Council purchased market rights from the Marquess of Salisbury in 1922.

Tommy remembers that *"it was only later when East End traders came that the cattle market was closed... The London people had fruit and vegetables and all sorts of clothing and general merchandise. I can remember there was one character called the Banana King who sold only bananas, and sold them by the hand. And he had a great patter, as most of these East End traders did."*

Although the main cattle market had disappeared from the High Street by the late 1940s, Les Riches recalls *"in the yard up the side of the Salisbury Arms there was a sort of livestock market – they used to have rabbits and guinea pigs, chickens and that sort of thing that you could buy."* George

The Cattle Market (1912)

Don has an admission to make. *"Us kids we used to run through there and nick the pins out of the cages and so the birds got out."*

HODDESDON FAIR

In the Middle Ages fairs always coincided with Saints Days, but quickly came to serve a mixture of religious and commercial purposes as the gathering together of a scattered rural population was a great opportunity for merchants and farmers to sell produce. By the 16th century the religious and commercial aspects had declined and been replaced by sideshows, rides, games, etc. In 1535 the current owner of market rights, Henry Bourchier, Earl of Essex, successfully petitioned the King for the date of the annual fair to be changed to the 3rd – 5th July.

In 1856, an anonymous resident wrote an evocative and detailed contemporary description of the festivities. *"Richardson's Theatre... usually occupied the space near the conduit pump. Great was the delight and noisy was the mirth, at the buffoonery on the platform between the well known clown and pantaloon, with their attendants Harlequin and Columbine... Under the colonnade of the Bull Inn might be seen the familiar faces of Mrs Rowley and others with attractive heaps of cherries from the local cherry orchards, and sundry choice viands, from pickled salmon to winkles. Roundabouts and swings and knock-em-downs with their tawny attendants received their share of attention."*

The report continues: *"In the fashionable hours of the afternoon, well dressed ladies and gentlemen of the neighbourhood paid state visits to the fair, and thoroughly enjoyed the mirthful scene. During the leisure hours of the evening, the windows of the neighbouring houses were decorated by the well-dressed and proverbially good-looking wives and daughters of tradesmen."* After dark both the Salisbury Arms and Bull Hotel held their own dances and *"high shoe balls."*

By the last decade of 19th century the Fair had become noisy and boisterous. Another account written by someone from the town says: *"The fair, in spite of our advanced civilisation, has lapsed into a scene of rowdyism more or less between the young of both sexes, alike disreputable and disgusting."* The event was initially moved to a field in Amwell Street and subsequently to Pound Close where it stayed as a popular annual fixture until the beginning of the current century. However, by 2010 there had been a noticeable decline in attendance and it moved back to its original location in the High Street. This proved a great success and now the Charter Fair is held annually in the town centre in October. *(see photo page 118)*

THE VICTORIA WINE COMPANY (122, High Street) currently Isabel Hospice Shop

If we now turn back to look at the east side of the High Street we see a large modern retail block with a small unit tacked on the side. If we had been here in 1963 on our left would have been the yard of Taylor Walker brewers and, appropriately located right next door, was a small branch of the Victoria Wine Company who ran a national chain of Off Licences.

Back in the 1930s the same shop was an off licence run by Edwin Dixon as the Cannon Stores stocking *'Taylor Walker Prize Beers'* – that company having become the new owners of the Cannon Brewery.

PRIVATE HOME (120, High Street) currently Specsavers and Savers

This large old house was the private residence of Mr Merchant, Chief Clerk of the Brewery at the end of the 19th century, and continued to be residential up to the mid 1960s when the ground floor was converted into a large single retail space for a Tescos supermarket, which later became the location of Bowman's general store. It was re-developed again recently, with additional flats above and behind, the ground floor split into two retail spaces and a small shop unit built slightly set back on the left.

THE WAR MEMORIAL

If we now turn to look over our shoulders we'll see the familiar site of the town's War Memorial. This was unveiled in a well-attended ceremony on

Remembrance Sunday at the War Memorial (1950s)

10th April 1921, despite suffering some minor damage when it fell over while being erected by workmen a few days earlier. Two additional commemorative slabs listing 40 local soldiers who died during World War II were unveiled on 29th July 1951.

A A BOND JEWELLERS (118, High Street) currently Garnier Jewellers

Back to the line of buildings in front of us today we see one of a run of small historic buildings which have miraculously survived into our century to continue serving as retail outlets. Paddick speculates: *"It is possible that Izaac Walton used this shop to buy fishing rods, lines, live and dead bait etc when he paid his many visits to the town."*

Just over a century ago this is listed as the home of Mrs Jane King, 'toy dealer', who had previously been ladies maid to famous Victorian hymn composer, Henriette Auber, at her home in Amwell Street. Hayllar remembers. *"When I was a boy it was a great delight to be given a penny to spend at 'Fanny' King's, who kept a funny little sweet and general shop."* Dorothy Chilton was regular visitor in the 1920s. *"The shops used to be open later on Saturday evenings and my father used to take me into town and I could buy one little piece for my toy farm from that shop – and they were lead pieces then."*

By the mid 1930s the shop housed Clarke's Grocery Store, *'Noted for finest English and Danish Bacon. Try our famous own make Pork Brawn.'* By the mid 1950s the town's well-established jewellers, A A Bond, had

A A Bond and Sons Jewellers (1963)

moved in from their previous location at the south end of town. *(see page 25)* They remained here for over three decades, changing their name to Bond & Sons before Garnier, a jeweller based in Fawkon Walk, moved the short distance across the High Street to take up residence in the 1990s.

STAGG'S BOOT SHOP (116, High Street) currently Maison Paul Restaurant

Behind here was the site of the town's original Almshouses built in 1440 to house five poor residents by local aristocrat, Richard Rich. Being very close to the boundary between the two neighbouring parishes of Broxbourne and Great Amwell their ownership was another cause for dispute. In 1834 these ancient homes were in good condition according to a report to the Charity Commissioners and still occupied by five poor families. However, the new Poor Law Act subsequently saw them sold off in 1841 for the substantial sum of £234.16s.1d.

By the late 19th century the building we see in front of us today was a boot and shoe maker run by Mrs. Emma Tricker, who appears to have taken

Staggs Boot Shop on left, Dymock plumbers centre and Brewster's butchers on the right (early 1930s)

over after the death of her husband. Stagg's Boot Shop moved across here from its original location on the west side of the street and Mr Harry Stagg took over the business after his father retired. In its early years the firm employed six men making riding boots, firemen's boots and special thigh-length boots for the sewer men who worked for Herts County Council.

Dorothy Chilton's family shopped there. *"I think Staggs really catered for heavier footwear – my father got his heavy boots – workman's type things. I remember Mr Stagg's son – he wore one of those brown overalls. He was dark, and he was rather well built and I think he was very interested in the swimming club."*

The building later housed Adam Kennedy's Estate Agency, before becoming the new home of furniture and gift shop Grayt Expectations who re-located from their premises at the south end of the High Street. In the last few years it has been transformed in quick succession into an artisan bakery and confectioners and then a French cafe, and has just been re-vamped yet again as a French restaurant.

DYMOCK'S PLUMBERS currently under construction

Some time in the 19th century this narrow house set back to the east was occupied by a plumbing, signwriting and decorating business run by Thomas Dymock. There are several members of the same family listed in a Trade Directory of the late 1890s. Arthur William was a pianoforte tuner also based in the High Street, Charles John was landlord of the Fox Inn a few doors down, Frank H was running the blacksmith's forge in Lord Street and Miss Mary A Dymock is listed as a dressmaker based in Amwell Street. By the inter-war period the plumbing business had moved to Lord Street. With the re-development of the Co-op store this house was demolished and an unsightly gap was left running alongside the northern wall of their building.

THE CO-OPERATIVE DEPARTMENT STORE currently under construction

Here we would have found two properties dating back to the late 16th century which were at one time inns: the White Hart and the White Horse. The former subsequently became known as *'John Cock at the Cross'*, probably because it was near the Market Cross and associated with the local Cok or Cock family. The gateway at the north end of this dwelling led down to the Common Marshes and in the late 16th and early 17th centuries was called *'Bolles Gate'* after a previous owner of the building, which itself had been known as 'The Rose'". A 'pindar' was based in a small room above the archway to check that anyone driving their livestock underneath was entitled to do so until access was closed off in 1569. The centre of the archway was the boundary between the parishes of Great

London Central Meat Company (late 1930s)

Amwell and Broxbourne. After these buildings were demolished in the early 1960s a boundary stone was placed in the pavement to mark the location.

LONDON CENTRAL MEAT COMPANY

The middle building was a fishmongers shop run by the Brewster family, possibly as early as the 1860s. By the late 1930s it had become a butchers owned by the London Central Meat Company managed by Alan Cook's uncle. *(see photo page 139)* Neville Townsend's family were patrons during the Second World War. *"It was the butchers with which we were registered for rations. This sometimes meant extra things like liver. The quality of such things was very variable, and I can remember my father being extremely annoyed about one consignment of liver that he considered very inferior because of the piping in it."*

A G COUSINS TOYSHOP

Perhaps not surprisingly this is one of the family run traders most vividly and fondly remembered by many older residents, like Dorothy Chilton. *"The toy shop was two storeys and rather a wobbly building near Staggs, next door to Brewsters – that was a lovely shop. They used to have dolls and train sets and books – everything, just the simple wooden toys – the 'use your imagination' sort of toys – tiddlywinks, jigsaws... We were taken in mainly on special occasions like birthdays and Christmas."* Peter Shepherd spent his pocket money there to buy *"dinky toys, which were, of course, my favourite in those days - and I think sixpence just about bought one."* George Don recalls *"the toys were all tinplate stuff ... lots were wind-up. And I remember seeing my first electric railway ever – it was just running in a circle."*

In the late 1930s the company had a second branch in Hoddesdon selling gift ware, and one in Hertford which included a furniture store. However, by 1944 Cousins had re-located to a new site at 77 High Street and this premises was filled by F E Gowers general stores.

By 1955 the buildings were in a dangerous state and were knocked down. A yawning hole was left behind wooden hoardings for several years until an ugly, out of place, two storey brick department store was eventually constructed by the Co-Operative in 1966 – on its first day and a half it took more money than the old Amwell Street store took in a week. It went on to trade very successfully in the town for almost another half a century.

But by the 21st century the store was struggling, and was sold, re-vamped and re-named 'Westgate' in 2006. In April 2008 the *Mercury* revealed:

"SHOCK waves rippled through Hoddesdon town centre this week as closure notices went up at the Westgate department store... The former Co-op department store was saved from closure just 18 months ago when it was bought by Anglia, but this week the group manager for the Westgate stores, Peter Golding, said: 'We tried but it is a commercial decision. The harsh reality is the store does not meet our commercial expectations.'"

After three years of wrangling over plans to re-develop the site by adding flats and an extended ground floor store the developer went into administration and the building was sold again to a local businessman. *'Revamp in Store for Landmark Hoddesdon Shop'* the *Mercury* headline announced on 22nd September 2011. *"PCL director, Joe Ricotta, said the intention was to bring the shop back into use as a retail outlet... 'We are going to redesign the whole site to make it look more decent,' he said. 'It's the ugliest building in Hoddesdon.' The priority for the new owners is to change the front of the shop."* At the time of writing in August 2014, following complete demolition of the old property, a sympathetically-designed, multiple-use development which comprises flats, a large retail unit and a restaurant is under construction.

WESTMINSTER BANK (106, High Street) currently Halifax Building Society

This was the site of another old Tavern - the White Swan. In a photo of the cattle market in 1887 the property appears to be split into a private residence on the north side with a shop next door, which in the 18th century was a 'peruke' maker who provided long wigs for fashionable gentleman of that period. Paddick reveals that: *"soon after the First World War it was re-fronted and greatly altered; the caretaker lived in the basement, the door of which was reached by means of area steps opening straight off the pavement."*

The Westminster Bank, which was in residence there in 1963, became the National Westminster after an amalgamation in 1968, which in its turn was swallowed up by Royal Bank of Scotland in 2000 leading to the 'rationalisation' of branches and the Halifax Building Society taking possession in their stead.

GOWERS GIFTWARE (104, High Street) currently Butlers Estate Agents

Split into two shops by the 1930s, glass and domestic wares were being sold in the left hand unit by Mrs Gower when Mary Young worked there

Westminster Bank and Gowers Giftware (1963)

after she left school. *"Mrs Gower was the manager and there was me and only one other staff – that was Hilda and I think she was the niece. Never been married, very timid, but a very nice lady. Mrs Gower didn't really work in the shop – she came in with her small dog... I never broke anything – she was very fussy 'don't touch anything, we don't want any breakages.'"*

GOWERS MENSWEAR (102, High Street) currently Prestige Bridal & Formalwear

This side of the property in the late Victorian period is called Market House and is the location of a 'tailor, outfitter and hosier' named James Batstone. Half a century later it is still selling menswear – this time under the auspices of Mr Gower who has offices on the floor above." By the 1980s Petite Fleur Bridals had become resident here, they in turn were supplanted by a carpet shop, but wedding wear is once again being sold and hired on the same premises today.

OLD BAKERIE SHOP (100, High Street) currently Equinox Jewellers

This charming old half-timbered building with an archway to the south

Tailor James Batstone standing outside his shop (c1890s)

was being used in 1886 by a butcher with the impressive Dickensian name of Stallabrass, who appears to have continued to operate there until at least the turn of the last century. The butcher's son subsequently worked at the Post Office for many years and was affectionately known as the 'singing postman' for his melodious voice which was heard and enjoyed on his rounds. In the last century the property served as Parker Brothers Bakery, which had become the Old Bakerie Shop by 1963.

GARDINERS (96–98, High Street) currently Hoddesdon Library

Another well-known and long established Hoddesdon independent trader was in business on this site for more than a century. Thomas Murray Gardiner set up shop here in 1863 – he also owned Burford House up near Boar's Head Inn where he operated a factory for the manufacture of sports equipment and children's playground rides. Tim Turner remembers seeing some of their kit. *"I saw a set of parallel bars in the gym at our school labelled 'Gardiner, Hoddesdon'."* Bicycles were made in a workshop next door to their store until the late 1920s.

Dorothy Chilton's father bought gardening items there. *"It was a wooden floor which was rather clattery and it was a bit dark and it always smelt of oil and they sold gardening things, tools and the staff wore those*

Gardiner's Ironmongers and Cycle Factory (late C19th)

brownish overalls. I think at one time they had sports equipment – tennis rackets, cricket bats - on one side."

Diana Borchards was fascinated by a female member of staff. *"I used to go to buy nails, screws, etc (by the pound) for dad and she would weight them out on an old fashioned 'see-saw' scale with weights and gather them to put in paper bag - but her nails were always bright red! They never had a mark on and looked immaculate... That shop was, to a small child, rather eerie to me - it was dark and cavernous with hidden parts. I was a great reader of Enid Blyton books and this reminded me of those."*

After the war Gardiners sold off the southern half their premises for the construction of a new Showroom for the Eastern Electricity Board. By the mid 1970s the shop had closed and their old building flattened to make way for another unattractive, functional block to house the town's new Library.

CHURCH'S DRESS SHOP (92 – 94, High Street) currently Cannon Travel and County Lettings

Our next stop is a charming property re-fronted with brick in the 18th century and the base for Mr Whitley the tailor between approx 1870 and 1900. By the mid 1930s Church's were listed as a 'drapers and milliners', but in the 1950s and 60s their adverts in the *Journal* had become decidedly racy: *'For that pretty, feminine look choose Kayser Bondor*

Fancy Pants. Lovely… lacy… frilly… and wonderfully long wearing from 8/11d.'

By 1963 they appear to have expanded into a small section of the property next door to their left. Around the turn of the century, Paddick writes, this little unit had previously been occupied by *"a Mr Griffin who sold and repaired clocks and watches and who visited the larger houses in the town winding clocks and keeping them in order under contract."* Before World War II watchmaker & jeweller, R C Saint was carrying on the same line of work. By the 1980s the main shop had become the Christos Bakery and Restaurant, while number 92 now contained 'Sew Easy' offering everything for the seamstress and embroiderer.

YE OLDE TUDOR CAFE (90, High Street) currently Appelman Charman Opticians

This ancient building, which from its architecture again seems likely to have served as an inn early in its long history, in the late Victorian period is occupied by Fruiterer John Barker, but by the late 1890s he has relocated to Lord Street. In the early years of last century Mr Ellis carried on his plumbers and builders business which was sold on to a certain Mr W J Haward in 1911 - of whom we shall hear a lot more shortly.

Just after World War I Thomas Knight Senior moved the Printers & Stationers business which he'd taken over in 1915, from the north end of the High Street *(see page 72)*. His eldest son Tommy tells the story. *"At the end of the war he commenced the business again by taking property at 90, High Street Hoddesdon. I was born there in 1920. We lived behind and above the stationery shop, which was in the front."*

When Mr Knight vacated this site to move his thriving company down to Brewery Road, the Tudor Tea Rooms opened to serve the townsfolk of Hoddesdon as one of their most popular eateries for more than 40 years. The owner was already one of the best known and most colourful personalities in the town: a certain Mr W J Haward, or 'Mr Hoddesdon' as he was nicknamed - the most prominent man in Hoddesdon from the 1930s through to the 1970s. According to George Don: *"Mr Haward lived in a house almost opposite where John Warner School is now. He was an ex-army man and my mother used to work for him, in the house, so many hours a week."*

The Haward family arrived in Hoddesdon from Rotherhide in 1880, shortly after their son was born. A profile in the first edition of the

A youthful Mr Haward and his wife go for a ride.

Hoddesdon Journal in 1935 revealed that their son Walter John *"was educated at the National School in Paul's Lane, under the late Mr J Fowler. At 15 years of age started work in the building trade in London and six years later started his own building business... He was elected to the Hoddesdon UDC in 1930... is also the Chairman of the Water Works Committee, Hoddesdon Traders Association, Hoddesdon Badminton Club, Argos F. C., and Hoddesdon Tennis Club."*

Virtually every one of my interviewees has anecdotes to share about this energetic local entrepreneur who continued to expand his business empire well into the 1950s. As Peter Shepherd puts it: *"He seemed to have an interest in most things, from the time you were born until the time you would die. He would have the café to feed you, the undertakers to bury you, the nursing home to bring you in to the world, the builders to build you a home, iron mongers and hardware shop to sell you things, so he seemed to have everything - oh, and a nursery also, to provide you with food."*

Arthur Wingate served Mr Haward regularly over the Post Office counter. *"He had a finger in every pie in Hoddesdon... I would say he was just an ordinary sort of man, not bombastic or anything. He wasn't pompous or arrogant or anything like that, he was just an ordinary, Hoddesdon man."* As a child Annette Marples found him an intimidating figure. *"He was very aware of who he was. I know sometimes my mum or dad used to say, 'When you go up the town, can you go in to Haward's and get...' you* know, you'd sort of look out and make sure he wasn't around because you didn't want to make a fool of yourself."

One of the wealthy Mr Haward's passions was motor racing, as the *Journal* reported. *"It is in the automobile line, however, that he has achieved most success. He acquired a motor bike in 1903 and in 1907 was one of the first persons in the district to possess a car. Entered for the Motor Trial Reliability for the first time in 1906 and since then has competed regularly, and today is holder of over 70 awards."*

Given his extensive business interests he employed a lot of local people, including Michael Dear who reveals that his old boss was called by the nickname 'Sparra' behind his back. *"'Sparra' was quite a character, he didn't throw his money about a lot because I remember one day, we had a workshop in Duke Street ... it was quiet, like the normal buzz, so I went in and said, 'I want the name of everybody who hasn't had a Christmas present.' No one said anything, so I repeated it again. Then, all of a sudden from behind these doors came Mr Haward himself. And he used to call everybody' laddy', so he said, 'You will have your little laugh, laddy, won't you?' Anyway, the next year we all got a Christmas bonus!"*

Haward's miserliness was legend, according to Peter Shepherd. *"I remember him once asking a lorry driver who delivered a load of bricks, some thousands of bricks, whether he would unload them as all his staff had left for the day. The chap said 'All right', loaded them off by hand, about half a dozen at a time and after about two or three hours work he'd finished. Haward proceeded to offer him sixpence - the man then told him*

Mr Haward in his sports car (late 1930s)

what he could do with his sixpence and threw it as far as he could possibly throw it... so not 'over generous', as I recall."

Even in old age he was as shrewd as ever, as Alan Cook confirms *"He was particularly interested in the Tower Centre, which he did not approve of at all. I remember him saying to my father, 'It's a white elephant, it will always be a white elephant, because the units are too small and it'll never be a real go.' And, of course, all these years later he was proven correct."* At the grand old age of 91 the town's most senior business personality was interviewed for a 1971 edition of the hugely popular BBC Radio series '*Down Your Way*' which demonstrated his hallmark gruffness and confirmed his lifelong reputation as a man of few words.

And so back to his Tudor Cafe – one of the town's social hubs, according to Diana Borchards. *"When mother met her friends for tea I would always ask to sit next to the walls which were panelled, and I would keep tapping on them when nobody was looking quite expecting a secret panel to slide open."* Even romances were kindled amongst the scones and caraway seed cake, as Brian Walsh recalls. *"My mother, when she first came to Hoddesdon worked for him in the Tudor Café - was manageress of the Tudor Café. And that is where my father and mother met, actually. She was serving him as a customer in the tea room."*

Interior Tudor Cafe (1940s)

Tucked away just behind the tea rooms, the ubiquitous Mr Hoddesdon also operated the Tudor Cafe Hall which became one of the town's premier entertainment venues during the Second World War. The young Mollie Muetzel spent many happy nights there. *"They used to have dances every Tuesdays, Fridays and Saturdays - sometimes, at one point, they were having them Thursdays as well. And of course I never missed one of those... All the soldiers used to come over from Hunsdon. The army used to come up from Hertford."* Just after the war Mollie met someone who, some years later, was to become her second husband. *"Peter, he was a German prisoner of war, and they kept them working in the greenhouses for two years after war. And then he came to the Tudor dance, and that's when we met first of all."*

Mr Haward built a brand new Tudor Hall in Conduit Lane which was completed in early 1955 and officially opened by none other than the super-star of the day, Arthur Askey. Of course, the *Journal's* representative was in attendance. *"With a crowd of about 450 people present, the new Tudor Hall, built by Mr W J Haward, was opened on February 11th. Characteristically Mr Haward took no part in the official proceedings. There can be no doubt the new Tudor Hall provides Hoddesdon with something for which there has been a crying need for many years, and the organisers of many functions larger than a good sized Sunday school party will no longer have the scratch their heads in dismay as they try to decide where they can find accommodation."*

Mary Young loved to dance in her teenage years. *"I remember Mr Haward coming in – yes, he used to come in – and I remember people saying 'Oh, he'll come and ask you for a dance'... He didn't know me, but if he came in he'd always come over and ask me for a quickstep. I don't think we ever spoke at all, that was the funny thing, but he was such a lovely quickstepper."*

Les Riches knew the venue as a place where a number of local bands performed live in front of enthusiastic fans. *"There was this group 'Tel Thorn and the Dwellers', a local group that used to play there. And they had a lead guitarist and he was fantastic, this guy."* Another band which played at the Tudor Hall and went on to enjoy some national fame at this time was Ray Dexter (real name Ray Kentish) and the Sunsets. They signed a record contract in September 1960 after appearing on the 'Caravan' entertainment programme on BBC Television and, having played to audiences on the Granada and Gaumont circuits, they were shortly off on a tour of service camps. In 1961 they released their first single called *'Coalman's Lament'*, written by Tommy Connor and produced by the famous Joe Meek.

Ray Dexter at the New Tudor Hall (Nov 1960)

By the early 21st century people's tastes and expectations for entertainment had radically changed and the rather run-down Hall had become a snooker club. It was demolished in 2012 to make way for a complex of flats, offices and retail units with a car park underneath.

SAMARITAN WOMAN

At this point on our tour we once again need to turn in the opposite direction to look back into the High Street and imagine a white stone fountain of a woman holding an urn that dominated the centre of the town's main thoroughfare for nearly 300 years. When he was building his impressive mansion on the southern fringes of the town, *(see page 169)*, Sir Marmaduke Rawdon went to the considerable expense of having piped water laid on from a spring over half a mile away. Finding this supply more than adequate for his personal needs, in 1631 he paid for a separate pipe to be laid to take water to the nearby town centre.

The 'Good Samaritan' or 'Diana', as she was also sometimes known, dispensed her vital supply for nearly 200 years. Tregelles takes up the story: *"In the course of time the head has lost power, partly no doubt from defects in the ancient leaden main pipe, which does not seem to have been*

Samaritan Woman and Town Pump (c1900)

renewed, though often patched, partly from defects in the brick enclosure of the spring, where much water goes to waste."

A more efficient and hygienic iron pump fed by an underground tank 30ft long, 9ft wide and 9ft deep with a lamp on top and a tap at the rear was subsequently installed in 1826. This survived for a century, until one foggy night in the 1930s when, Hayllar tells us, *"a car driven by Viscount Gladstone's chauffeur collided with it and so badly damaged it that it had to be taken down and replaced by a drinking fountain on the pavement."*

The Samaritan Woman initially found refuge in the butcher's yard on the west side of the High Street run by the Tuck family, during which time it was further damaged by local boys using it for target practice. In 1894 plans were put forward, with strong support from C P Christie, for the statue to be re-erected in the High Street, but it was deemed beyond repair. She was removed to the Council's sewage works in Rye Park and abandoned to her fate.

In the 1930s several prominent local residents again lobbied to get the Samaritan Woman rescued and repaired – a major job, as Mr Paddick explains, since the statue *"was found to be in a very bad state, covered with the dirt of 109 years, the head severed from the body, the nose broken from the face. Various holes had been made in the body through which odd pipes had been inserted."* In 1937 the statue was successfully restored by the renowned sculptor Charles Giddings who lived locally.

Hoddesdon UDC announced its intention to place the statue on a grand plinth at the front of its new District Council Offices. However, this was never implemented, so instead she languished for over 30 years in the back yard of the building before being shunted into obscurity in the mid 1980s under a clump of trees in the garden of Lowewood Museum where she remains today. Proposals to have her moved back to a prominent spot into the town centre in recent years have, so far, come to nothing.

SYMES SPORTS (88, High Street) currently the Eye Gift Shop and Miami Carpets

Let's now turn back to the east side of the High Street where we find ourselves looking at another attractive half-timbered property which was once the Fox Inn – another hostelry tied to the Christie Brewery. By the inter-war years the pub had been replaced by Newman's restaurant with a club room at the rear, advertising itself as 'the cyclists rest' which Dorothy Chilton knew well. *"Mr Newman had the little café next to Bristows and they also sold sheet music. Their son ran a cycle shop in Burford Street – he was a fireman."* By the early 1960s the property was

Newman's Restaurant (c1930s)

split into two on the ground floor with a cafe on the left side and Symes Sports outlet on the right.

BOBBIE'S FASHIONS (86, High Street) currently Rickmores Electrical Centre.

This corner block appears to have once been an extension to the Fox Inn which subsequently became a Drapers run first by Mr Cherry and then Fred Gurney who had his name emblazoned on the fascia in gorgeous copperplate lettering. *(see photo page 149)* Just after the Great War it was taken over in turn by a Mr Ernest Bristow who came from Lewisham to Hoddesdon in 1921 to run his 'drapers and outfitters' shop. He was elected to the Hoddesdon UDC in 1924 and served for many years in different capacities. In the *Journal* in 1935 he is reported as being very active on behalf of the local fire brigade and serving as Secretary of the Hoddesdon & District Traders Association. His hobbies are listed as fishing, gardening and bowls.

When Mr Bristow died suddenly in August 1939 the *Journal* ran an obituary. *"His kindly disposition and earnest desire to do right by his fellow citizens was manifest in all his activities, and it was his delight to serve in an official capacity for any event of public importance."* He had helped to organise the recent Golden Jubilee celebrations, the Coronation Carnival and the Chamber of Commerce's annual 'Shopping Weeks'.

In the 1950s William Smith tells us, the new occupant was *"the Co-operative gown shop - which was on the corner of Conduit Lane, which my aunt was the Manager of. She was a very fashionable lady - very well presented."* Bobbie's boutique was frequented by fashion-conscious teenager Mary Young. *"In the 1950s they used to have the dresses with the underskirts stiffened. It was quite expensive in there, but it was nice stuff. And you used to be able to go in there and pick something out and leave a deposit and they'd hold it. Because in those days we couldn't always pay the whole lot straight away."*

HIGH STREET PEDESTRIANISATION

Standing on the north corner of Conduit Lane we have to take another pause and look back up the stretch of the High Street we have just traversed so that we can cover the controversial and stormy tale of how the town was blighted by arrogant town planners in the 1980s.

The construction of a bypass to the east of the town in the 1960s, followed in 1972 by the building of the £5m A10 dual carriageway to the west had proved a mixed blessing for Hoddesdon. Whilst it took away the volume of heavy traffic which was now clogging up the town centre, it also diverted drivers round the back of the High Street and away from the town itself. In 1977 Pevsner sardonically observed: *"The tortuous new traffic scheme illustrates the difficulty of imposing vehicle segregation on a town which owes its existence to being on a main road."*

In the mid 1980s Broxbourne Council gave the go-ahead for building of the first phase of a large out-of-town shopping centre at Brookfield Farm, just a few miles down the A10 from Hoddesdon. Co-incidentally, just as this development was nearing completion in 1987, the Council revealed their intention of creating a pedestrian zone at the north end of Hoddesdon High Street. Alarmed traders and residents attended a public meeting called by the Hoddesdon Society and Chamber of Commerce in October 1987. Warnings were issued by several speakers that banning car parking from half the High Street meant the town "*would be killed stone dead.*"

Paying no attention to the objections and ignoring alternative suggestions put forward by the local organisations, draft proposals were issued by Broxbourne Council in a glossy brochure the following year with the name of the Mike Walker, Director of Planning and Environment, very noticeable on the front cover.

A planner's utopian vision of Hoddesdon High Street when pedestrianised (1960s)

On the basis that *'existing traffic management restrictions in the High Street are being widely abused and most shops lack adequate servicing arrangements'*, the only solution was to bulldoze new service roads along the rear of the shops at the north end of the street, introduce a one way system, ban access for private vehicles, and block off the east end of Lord Street. This would allow for the pedestrianisation of the area and the banning of all car parking in this section of the town centre although, astonishingly, large buses and local taxis would still be allowed to drive through.

The retailers and residents mounted a valiant campaign against the plans which the *Mercury* revealed in September 1989 proved there was *'a landslide of public opinion'* against it – 2500 people had signed a petition objecting to the project, in addition to 126 official representations and over 100 letters and articles in the local press. The campaign successfully pressed for a Public Enquiry on the plans, but when the Government Inspector's Report was published in August 1989 it was ambiguous enough to allow the Council to sweep aside all the criticisms and forge ahead.

Brain Walsh, owner of Meadows, was involved in the campaign. *"People were quite prepared to jump on the bus and get their products and carry them all home. That was the thing – pave over the High Street, do away with the parking spaces. There was a campaign to stop that, there was a Public Enquiry which was held in St Paul's Church and the public enquiry came down on the side of the retailers."* The only concessions made by the Council were that the scheme would be introduced in three phases, and they promised that new free car parks would be created to compensate for the loss of parking spaces in the pedestrian areas.

By the end of 1991 the town was in turmoil as the consequences of the first phase of the town centre re-modelling became apparent. On 9th November the *Mercury* reported that *"anger and frustration... reached boiling point on Monday when more than 350 townspeople gathered for a stormy public meeting. Despite high winds, torrential rain and just three days' notice Hoddesdon Parish Church was packed to the rafters – such was the depth of feeling. And speaker after speaker stood up to denounce not only the ongoing Phase 1 enhancement scheme but also the initial decision by Broxbourne Council to introduce it."*

An even more volatile meeting attended by more than 250 people followed a month later - owners of the many independent shops were furious that the Council had suddenly introduced car parking charges in all the town's car parks, whilst the enormous car park at nearby Brookfield Farm would still remain free of charge.

Brian Walsh still feels the people of the town were deceived by Broxbourne Council. *"To this day I feel annoyed really. When Brookfield Farm development went ahead – Tescos and M&S and that sort of thing, the Council did say to us that they would never impose parking charges in Hoddesdon because there was free parking down there. That was what we understood – I wouldn't like to stand up in a court of law and say that, but that was what was said to us. And, of course, when they did introduce parking charges it did have a detrimental effect on our business."*

Attending the meeting was Mike Walker, the architect of the scheme, who had now been swiftly promoted to Chief Executive of the Borough – a post he was to hold for almost another quarter century. According to a *Mercury* article he *'apologised if the council had given the impression they had come for a fight and said it comes to listen and understand as clearly as possible any comments you have got.'*

Having listened, Broxbourne Council then simply steamed ahead with the rest of the scheme as the business owners and residents fought an increasingly frustrating rearguard action which was completely ignored. For Brian Walsh this was the final straw and he decided the time had come to sell up and get out. *"The parking charges probably took away 10% of our business and the pedestrianisation another 10%. And we were also under pressure from the supermarkets and we just couldn't see a light at the end of the tunnel."* The family sold their delicatessen in the mid 1990s and today, ironically, their premises are owned and run by their former arch-rival Tesco.

Another serious blow came in 1997 with the announcement that a barrier system using rising bollards was going to be installed to keep out all traffic, bar the few delivery lorries that had to gain access to the handful of businesses that had no rear access - but even they were only permitted entry before 10am or after 4pm.

It was to take more than a decade before another high profile public campaign organised by the *Action for Hoddesdon* group of business owners and residents finally forced Broxbourne Council into a U turn at the cost of another £90,000 of local ratepayer's money. At the beginning of December 2009 the hated bollards were permanently lowered to allow free flow of cars back into the north end of the High Street where 23 free parking spaces had been created.

However, Mike Walker, still at the helm of the Authority when this victory of common sense was finally achieved, was not destined to remain in position for much longer. On 2nd May 2013 the *Mercury* broke the exclusive news that Mr Walker had suddenly and unexpectedly *"been*

East side of the High Street with Conduit Lane before widening (1963)

granted *'special leave'* while the authority considers changing its management structure... Last month Mr Walker was criticised for signing off a letter in support of a drugs centre in Waltham Cross." A few months later the former Chief Executive was gone, having apparently left his post by *'mutual agreement'* and receiving a £100,000 compensation payment.

CONDUIT LANE

If we now just glance down Conduit Lane today we see a wide modern thoroughfare, quite a contrast to the narrow and densely wooded lane which had been there a century before. Two shops were knocked down in the 1960s to widen the road – the corner site was a small Barber's shop for nearly 70 years, initially run by Mr C A Elphee, where George Don later went to get his hair cut by Mr Gibson. *"He had a goldfish in a bowl in the window... It was only a little square room."*

Next door at number 82 Mrs. Eliza Brewster was trading as a fishmonger in the late 1890s. Several decades later the family re-appear on the High Street in new premises at the northern end next to the Parish Church. Just before the First World War this is where Batsfords are now running their poulterer and fishmonger's shop. A fishmonger and greengrocery store run by the Brill family served the local community here from the 1930s to the 1960s. It seems entirely appropriate, I suppose, that someone dealing in fish should have had a passion for teaching swimming, according to Annette Marples. *"The open air pool - that's where I learnt to swim, but it was much smaller than the one that was closed... Mrs Brill, they used to have a fruit shop. She was so strict; I used to swim with my head above the water, and she'd come along and push my head right under."*

HAYWARD'S IRONMONGERS (78, High Street) currently Langley Dry Cleaners

The ironmongers store opened here in October 1936 as another outpost of the sprawling Haward corporate empire, with a special offer of two shillings in the pound discount on all cash purchases. It also acted as the base for his booming building business. The shop was still trading as W J Haward as late as 1987, after its founder had passed on. In the last couple of decades it has seen a variety of retailers come and go.

STANBOROUGHS (76, High Street) currently due for refurbishment

We now find ourselves standing admiring a rather fine timber-framed mansion which has clearly seen better days. It takes its name from Thomas Stanborowe, a horse dealer, who occupied a house on the site in 1363 and, according to court roles: *"habitually overburdened the common grazing with his animals."*

Gibson's Barbers and Brills Greengrocers & Fishmongers (1963)

In 1605 it was owned by Robert Mitchell who built the oldest part of the present house in the mid 17th century, as Tregelles recounts. *"The house, although not so well built as Rawdon House, has some fine features; the turret stairs and long wing rooms are good... Of late years part of it was occupied as a training home for servant girls under the auspices of various ladies including, in especial, Miss Faithfull, daughter of a Rector of Hatfield."*

In 1900 it became the headquarters of the Hoddesdon and Broxbourne Unionist Club where prominent Conservative townsmen *"might meet in a social atmosphere,"* according the Club's Jubilee Celebration Booklet of 1950. We also learn that the Trustees paid the Christie Brewery £80 for the provision of electric lighting from its own generating plant *"and the Club was therefore one of the first premises to be lighted by electricity in the town."* For the first decade financing the upkeep of the organisation was a constant challenge and subscriptions were increased and social functions organised to raise funds.

This wasn't their only problem: *"In the early days of the century rivalry between the Conservatives and Liberals – the only political parties in those days – was very strong in the town and at one election members of the Club were forced to barricade themselves in the Club premises, which were being stormed by the Liberals, all the windows being smashed from the street."*

Period engraving of the rear of Stanboroughs

At some time in the latter half of the last century the Conservative Club, as they'd become, were allowed to obscure the fine architectural features at the rear of the property with an unsightly function room on stilts and completely cover up the main entrance with a hideous modern toilet block. Thankfully these additions have both been removed in the current re-development of the site which has seen a new clubhouse built on the car park at the rear, with a block of flats to follow.

Stanboroughs itself has been earmarked for an estimated £1m of renovation work to be carried out before it is sold on for commercial use, possibly as a restaurant. One very much hopes that the wood panelled room on the first floor containing a rare carved 17th century fireplace and the wooden turret staircase leading to it will be preserved intact in the process.

In 1939 the ground floor of the building was converted into two retail units and Wright & Mills: Herts County Opticians had moved in to the northern one. In the 1960s the southern unit was home to Lea Carpets Ltd. At some point before the millennium the ground floor was re-incorporated into the building to serve as a front bar for party members.

SHARP CHEMISTS (74) currently empty pending re-development

This was the private dwelling of Mr Rowe, manager of Hare's grocery shop opposite, for some 70 years. The first 'chymist' shop was opened

Stanborough's turret staircase and 17th century wooden fireplace (1950)

here around 1907 by Mr Postlethwaite, and independent chemist's Sharp continued to serve the local population from the early 1960s until just after the turn of this century.

POST OFFICE (72, High Street) currently the same

Before 1893 this was the site of a charming old fashioned, bow-fronted general store operated by Tuck and Sinclair selling Berlin wool, cottons, ribbons, etc., which Tregelles describes as *"typical of the Hoddesdon of 1700 or thereabouts."* The confident Victorian building we now see was designed by none other than architect John Allen Tregelles, who was later to write the first history of the town, and built by John Alfred Hunt.

Henry John Ashford took the job of Postmaster in July 1870 with a salary of £55 per annum - by 1893 he had moved his staff across to their new purpose-built premises and was also 'Registrar of Births, Deaths and Marriages for the Hoddesdon District'.

Arthur Wingate started work there as a trainee in October 1939. *"I was under training with Mr Durrant - a lovely man, he'd been there a long while, and he took me under his wing and he looked after me... the training consisted of work on the counter, an awful lot of sorting because of all the number of firms, large firms, that evacuated out of London to Hoddesdon."* At that time all the functions of the Post Office were contained in the same building - the sorting office was behind where the main counter still is today; upstairs was the telegraph and telephone exchange, along with about 30 postmen.

According to her stepson, Mrs Kathleen Langridge became Head of the Telephone Exchange in the 1930s, causing a bit of a stir as she was the first woman in the country to hold that post. He also tells the story that apparently the first telephone line connected to the Hoddesdon Exchange was for a bookmakers in Naezing.

BRIDGEMAN & SON ESTATE AGENTS (70, High Street) currently Paul Wallace Estate Agents

The first dwelling on this site belonged to Agnes Gamblyn back in 1522; in 1704 it had become the Crown and Mitre Inn, later re-named the Rose and Crown, which was demolished in 1842.

By the turn of the 20th century it served as the offices of Bridgeman & Son Auctioneers, Surveyors, Estate Agents, Valuers. In the 1930s they were advertising properties on the new Westfields Residential Estate – it cost £775 for a detached property with a garage, or £675 for a semi-detached house requiring a minimum deposit of £50.00. The business carried on after the war, but run by Timothy Blanchflower. In the 1970s W H Lee & Co are operating their Estate Agency here, only to be subsequently replaced by Paul Wallace who still occupy the premises today.

MONTAGUE HOUSE (68, High Street) currently Lloyds Bank

This grand Georgian mansion is the former home of one of Hoddesdon's most famous citizens – the pioneering 19th century road builder and engineer, John McAdam. He experimented on his own estate and in several government posts with ways to improve road construction, during which time he travelled over 30,000 miles of road and spent over £5,000 of his own money. In 1815 he became Surveyor of Bristol's roads and put his inventions into practice with great success. This led to his appointment as Surveyor General for the whole country in 1827 by which time he had moved to live in Hoddesdon, where he stayed until his death in 1836.

WHITING'S ANTIQUE SHOP (66, High Street) currently for sale for £1.3m

Another impressive 18th century construction, with a grand pedimented doorway hidden away down a narrow alleyway on the south side. For many years in the 20th century it was the home of the Hodson family until their last surviving daughter died in 1955. Tim Turner, who now is one of

East side of the High Street with (left to right) the Post Office, Montague House and Whiting's Antiques (1979)

Sworder's team of auctioneers, was fascinated by the antique shop run here by Mrs Whiting in the late 1950s. *"There used to be a concrete step the whole way along the front of the shop which I used to stand on to look in the windows."* A modest and tasteful sign was still identifying this smart address as an antique emporium in 1979.

HOGGES HALL (64, High Street) currently Kirby Colletti Estate Agents and Pepper & Phillips Funeral Directors

This is the site of a much older property which in 1086 was the Manor House of Mandeville and, at a later date, was called 'Haukes Vill'. Tregelles continues: *"Hogges Hall... has much heavy oak timbering of a fine character, and is probably fourteenth century work, possibly the oldest house in the town."* There are still some exposed timbers that can be seen in the ground floor offices of Kirby Colletti, plus a beautiful Victorian stained glass window at the back of the internal staircase.

John Alfred Hunt who was born in 1846 lived here and took on his father's builder's business in 1869, which he then expanded rapidly. The firm built St Catherine's Estate in 1883, St Cuthbert's Church in Rye Park, All Saints Church in Hertford, and many other private and public buildings all over the country. In the 1890s he is described as 'builder and contractor, brick maker and lime burner'. He became an original member of Hoddesdon UDC, was appointed a JP and later a permanent magistrate.

From the 1930s to 1970s this warren of a building housed a radio, electrical and music shop run by W R Stone. Their December 1936 advert reads: '*Christmas will be all the merrier if you have music and we can fit you up and supply you with all the latest records for the Gramophone or Radiogram.*' In the 1950s Mr Stone served as the President of Hoddesdon Rotary Club.

Next door in the same building in the 1930s was Stella Ladies Outfitters, selling women's underwear, hosiery, gowns and coats. By the end of the decade it had become home to John Howarth Footwear. By the 1960s footwear was still on sale there, but now offered by Coleman's shoe shop. In 1935 the southern end of the property housed L E Porter specialising in '*Art Needlework and Wools with hand knitted goods a speciality*'. By 1947 the shop had changed hands and was trading as Eve Smith. In 1955 the Vanity Box Ladies & Childrens Hairdressing salon was under the supervision of Sheila M Ruthven and Irene A Goodsell, where you could have '*permanent waving*' or '*dyeing and tinting at moderate prices.*'

60-62 High Street (1930s)

HUNT'S OFFICES (60 – 62, High Street) currently Tandoori Nights Indian Restaurant and Captain Cod Fish & Chips.

Mr Hunt constructed this new building for company offices, Mr Paddick informs us, there had previously been *"an old house probably dating from 17th century, its roof undulating with age, and owing to the imbalance of its windows, it had a somewhat peculiar look from the street. It had been built as one dwelling, but had later been divided into two."*

Between 1925 and 1936 these became the offices of the Hoddesdon UDC before they moved in to their new purpose-built HQ at the south end of the town. Subsequently Geoffrey Hunt & Co (Insurance) and Hoddesdon Land Company (Estate Agents) moved into number 62, with C A Bryant's Corn and Seed Merchants re-locating from their shop opposite to set up next door .

LOVEDAYS (58E, High Street) currently the Co-operative Bank

This was the location of very ancient building known in a deed of 1403 as 'The Cross Keys', or 'The Key'; by 1485 we know its letting value was eight shillings and four pence. By the early 20th century this has gone, and in the gap left we'd have found a large pair of gates in the 1930s advertising *'Loveday's Second Hand Furniture and Antiques. To make your Home a Home Sweet Home'*. They offered a whole range of household services: re-upholstering, French polishing, furniture repairs, picture framing, floor staining, etc. Their removals service used *'super modern motor pantechnicons.*

One of Les Riches' family was employed by the firm after the war. *"It wasn't a shop so much as a lock-up. My Uncle Cyril... used to do a lot of French polishing still for Lovedays."* Mary Young's mother worked in the company office, *"So I used to always go in there when I came out of school. I loved it as they had a couple of big sheds with everything, books, and you could just potter around and look at everything. It was like an open yard and at the end was the office. Then the owner went to Hertford and opened Beckwiths Antiques."*

The gap left was eventually filled towards the end of the last century by a new building sympathetically designed to blend in seamlessly with its surroundings.

From left to right – Lovedays, Herts Circulating Libraries and Alice Nicholls florist (1930s)

HERTS CIRCULATING LIBRARIES + ALICE NICHOLLS (58, High Street) currently Nationwide Building Society

In yet another imposing Georgian house next door which continued to be called 'The Key' we find the ground floor split into two shops. In the mid 1930s at 58B the Herts Circulating Libraries are offering romantic novels for just 2d, whilst 'floral designer and fruiterer' Alice Nicholls is trading next door for the next two decades. *(see page 113)*

RATHMORE HOUSE (56, High Street) currently Duffield Harrison

John Borham built the present mansion – his initials and date 1746 are in the framework over the very impressive Queen Anne style doorway. Tregelles tells the tale of its history. *"The original tenement was bequeathed by some owner, name unknown, to the Guardians of the (St Katherine's) Chapel, and was held by them for the town until the old house tumbled down in 1693. In 1743 the ground was let by the parish to John Borham, mealman, for ninety nine years at £1 per annum."*

Since the mid 19th century this property has been know as the 'Doctor's House', having served as a surgery for more than 100 years. The first medical owner was Dr James in the Regency period; Dr Robert Ingram Stevens was working there at the end of the century. Hayllar remembers him as a *"fine, bearded figure, always immaculately dressed in frock coat and top hat, going his rounds in a Brougham with coachman."*

Rathmore House to the left with old Esdaile House in centre (c1890s)

The very well known and popular GP, Dr Leonard West, operated his practice here from 1907 to his death in 1945. He was a JP, County Councillor and member of the Hoddesdon UDC. In the First World War he served with the Royal Army Medical Corps, and then became Medical Officer of Hoddesdon's Civil Defence Services in 1939.

John Gervis joined the practice of Drs Beilby and Roe based here in 1959. *"We ran a GP surgery, accessible seven days a week. Surgeries were morning and evening with no appointments necessary, together with afternoon clinics. Ann Cayford was our chief receptionist - a wonderful lady who used to bicycle in from Cheshunt each day. She was aided by Susan Clark and Ann Jones. A small office housed all the practice records. Freddy Beilby's consulting room was at the back of the house with a nice view of the garden. We used to enjoy our morning coffee and smokes there! On the middle floor resided Annie Stamp, the house keeper, and her husband Bill. Leslie Roe lived on the top floor."* Their premises having becoming too small, the practice moved out around 1970 to a new clinic in the Hoddesdon Health Centre.

At this point we pause where the line of properties comes to a sudden and unnatural halt and we are confronted by the roar of traffic as cars stream past on to Carlton Way in the direction of Hoddesdon's over-abundance of supermarkets. To make way for the inevitable and inexorable needs of the private motorist a tranche of old properties which appear in the old photo *(page 164)* were bulldozed in the early 1960s. They included a

Interior of the newly built St Augustine's Church (1962)

double- fronted two storey building, with a central entrance to a shop and side entrance to the house; and a pair of cottages built in 1869 to replace two low, ramshackle dwellings with an overhanging gable probably dating from mid 16th century.

ESDALE HOUSE currently St Augustine's Catholic Church

Next came the site of Esdaile House, another Georgian pile named after James Esdaile who lived there around 1800. It was demolished in 1878 by brewery magnate, Charles Peter Christie, to build his own detached, double-fronted Victorian villa which was named Esdale House - the new spelling apparently attributed to a typo by a lawyer's clerk. According to the sales particulars of 1913 this *'very valuable and important property... in the old world town of Hoddesdon'* contained 18 bed and dressing rooms, entrance and spacious lounge halls, five reception rooms, a conservatory, stabling for five horses plus five acres of *'pleasure grounds and paddock'*.

By 1932 this now very unfashionable old house was purchased by the Catholic Church and became St Augustine's Priory. It was pulled down in the early 1960s to make way for the construction of St Augustine's Catholic Church which opened in August 1962.

Esdale House from the garden (1913)

If we cross the main road here and turn right we find ourselves at the narrow entrance to Esdaile Lane on the left which ran along the south side of the new church and was one of the ancient entrances to South Field just behind. Formerly known as South Lane, in the mid 19th century for some years it was called School Lane and access to it was blocked at its junction with the High Street by a five barred gate.

ESDAILE HALL

This was the site of the original British School for Boys built by John Warner in 1841 which only served the town for a few years before being superseded by the National School in Paul's Lane. In the early 20th century the building became known as Esdaile Hall and was hired out as a function hall for public meetings and all sorts of social and charity events. Neville Townsend elaborates: *"The British Legion had premises in Esdaile Hall - they had a bar, and also a hall with a stage. My parents used to go there for whist drives and beetle drives, not to mention jumble sales. We performed our Scout Gang Show there too."*

It also served as the main venue for performances by the Hoddesdon Players Amateur Dramatic Society in the post-war period, which included Mary Newton among their members. *"Well, it was quite an experience to put a play on in the Esdaile Hall because, for starters, the stage was not in the centre of the hall it was stuck to one side of it, in the corner. It was*

Esdaile Hall (late 19th century)

extremely small - I should say it might have been 9 feet by 12 feet - and you could just about comfortably get a small sofa, perhaps an armchair, and a table on. But we used to perform, of course, on this. And the trouble was, of course, being in the corner of the Hall there was only one exit or entrance, and that was stage left."

This meant that if a performer had to exit to the right of the stage but come back on from the opposite side, they had to scramble out of a 3 foot square trapdoor located about four feet up on the rear wall, then run all the way round the back and through the billiard room to re-appear on cue. *"I always say that that was jolly good training"*, says Mary, *"because if you could appear on stage having hared round the back of a building, perhaps in the pitch black and rain, climbed up on to a chair, got through a three foot hole in the wall, and appear all calm and collected - now that was acting! In fact, we became known as the 'hole in the wall gang'."*

During the same period the Hall was used for the showings of the annual *'Hoddesdon Newsreel'* which was produced by local filmmaker, Tom Franklin. His close friend Tommy Knight explains that *"quite early on after the war he started doing cinematography... and he went off to film any event that looked as though it was of local interest. So every year he produced a newsreel and a holiday film... for charity, for the Peoples Dispensary for Sick Animals."* Alan Cook loved the shows; *"we'd go in, sit down, and then Tom would start with an introduction and start the film show and that was about it really, because there wasn't sound in those days - it was silent and Tom would occasionally put in a little bit of narration."* By the mid 1950s over 1,000 locals were watching themselves, friends and family on the big screen each year - adults were being charged 1/6d and children's tickets cost 9d.

Having been based at Esdaile Hall since 1947 the British Legion re-located to new offices in the Tower Centre in 2003. In September 2005 the *Mercury* carried a report on the fate of their former home. *"Fire has torn through the derelict 19th-century former British Legion Hall, gutting the building and destroying the roof, in an incident which mirrors an almost identical blaze there 18 months ago."*

The carved coping stone which recorded the original use of the building as a school disappeared in the aftermath of the blaze but was recovered from a workman by Hoddesdon Rotary Club member, Meirion Morris, and later it was donated to John Warner School in Stanstead Road where it is on display in their reception area today. The remains of the hall were recently re-developed as private flats.

A British Legion fundraiser at Esdaile Hall (1960s)

RAWDON HOUSE

Rawdon House, which in earlier times was called Hoddesdon House, is the oldest, largest and grandest house in the town, set back from the main road here at the south end of the High Street. Hayllar describes it as *"the architectural lion of the district."* The projecting porch still has the Rawdon arms over the doorway and on the little seen east or garden front is a square tower rising above the roof.

It was probably built some time in the early 1620s by Sir Marmaduke Rawdon who was a very wealthy merchant adventurer and confidant of both James I and Charles I. He became an MP, and later one of the Lieutenant Colonels of the City of London. During the Civil War he fought bravely on the Royalist side, particularly at the siege of Basing House where he beat off a large Parliamentary force which earned him a knighthood from the king, before dying of a sudden illness in 1646.

His connection with our town was established when he wooed and won Elizabeth Thorowgood who lived in Hoddesdon - the daughter and heiress to her father's considerable fortune with a handsome dowry of £10,000. After his father in law died, Marmaduke inherited the family home and replaced it with an imposing mansion in the latest architectural style. The marriage appears to have been a happy and successful one, with the couple producing ten sons and six daughters, eight of whom survived into adulthood. In 1624 he also took in his nephew, known as Marmaduke the Traveller, after the early death of his brother.

Sir Marmaduke clearly enjoyed entertaining at his luxurious home – James I was a regular visitor travelling to and from his palace of Theobalds near Cheshunt and his favourite hunting lodge at Royston. His wife Elizabeth was reputed to have had a 'smoking room' – later known as the summer house – built in the grounds which smokers were expected to use as the King detested smoking to such an extent that he had written a pamphlet condemning the practice.

Paddick tells us: *"In 1734 Robert Plomer... married Hester, daughter of the last of the Marmaduke Rawdons to reside in Hoddesdon, as the result of which the Rawdon finances were re-established on a firm footing, the family having been much impoverished by the sacrifices made for King Charles by the founder of the Hoddesdon Rawdons in the Civil War of 1642-6."* The Rawdon family continued to live at Rawdon House until 1740, after which time the house was let privately.

John Warner purchased the property in 1840 and it became a school for girls run by Mr Warner's great friend Mrs Ellis between 1845 and 1865. Mr Henry K Ricardo bought the property in 1875 and undertook a major restoration programme in 1879 which involved adding a whole new wing to create a luxurious private home. In a May 1969 *Mercury* article Edward Paddick writes that *"some older residents of Hoddesdon remembered sleighs of the Ricardo sons being driven around the district during snowy*

Eastern front and gardens of Rawdon House (c1900)

winters, their bells a tinkle in the frosty air."

According to a description by John Hunt, owner of Hoddesdon's leading building firm, in a lecture he delivered to the East Hertfordshire Archaeological Society at their AGM in 1902, the grounds of the house were still both extensive and impressive. *"The garden on the east side is all that an old garden should be, an old terrace wall supporting the upper garden. And below it a broad border full of rare flowers, the result of many year's collection; well kept yew hedges of great height, with long straight paths between; many beautiful old trees, a mulberry of exceptional growth, and the never-forgotten fountain."*

The mansion was purchased by Mr C P Christie in 1892 who, having retained a portion of the grounds adjacent to his new house, subsequently sold it on in 1898 to Miss White. She donated her new property to nuns to set up the Convent of the Order of the Canonesses Regular of StAugustine presided over by Rev Mother Prioress Southwell. It later became known by locals as St Monica's Priory.

Mr Tregelles was not impressed by the new owner's use of this fine building. *"Nearly the whole of its best oak panelling and all the fine chimneypieces have been removed and sold; a glaring corrugated iron structure forms an incongruous adjunct to the wing built by Mr Ricardo, and the venerable appearance of the mansion is sadly spoiled."*

Entrance Hall of Rawdon House (c1890s)

Up until 1959 the sisters were confined to the grounds and never seen by anyone outside the Order. According to a *Mercury* reporter in 1968: *"It had on the acres of land behind the priory, a herd of cattle for milk. There were vegetable gardens for food. The nuns baked their own bread; they spent their time in prayer and contemplation. And when they died they were buried simply in part of the grounds set aside for this. Now they have no cattle; they shop in local supermarkets; they travel on local buses... the ever increasing costs of living have finally forced the nuns – with the utmost reluctance – to try and sell the priory."*

The dozen remaining nuns departed in 1969 after a long battle with Hoddesdon UDC who refused to give planning permission for housing to be built on the site estimated to be worth £250,000. It was sold off instead to a property developer who proposed plans to demolish it in 1970. These were defeated after a successful campaign masterminded by former Librarian and local historian, Edward Paddick - but permission was given for a large housing estate to be built in the grounds. The mansion was acquired by the Beadle Group in 1973, sympathetically renovated and converted into offices which were completed in 1975.

COFFIN HOUSES (48-50, High Street) currently Priory Close

Tregelles describes the two unusual properties that once stood here as *"a pair of houses of ancient aspect whose upper storey overhangs the footway. Here in 1605 stood a house called 'The Elm', sometimes 'The Tree'... and the name points to the presence of large trees in the street before 1600."* The building was sub-divided into two dwellings - the southern one called Yew Arbour became the home of local historian, Mr Alexander McKenzie, who was appointed the first Clerk of the new Urban District Council. Mr Paddick tells us that the property was *"reputed to be haunted by 'The Lady in Green' and thirty years ago many well known people of the town were convinced they had seen her."*

Plans to demolish this building in the late 1950s, by then known as the 'coffin houses', caused much local opposition when it was discovered there were plans to replace them with a nine storey block of modern flats. Despite a plea from the renowned poet Sir John Betjeman that the buildings be protected, when the scale of the new development at Priory Close was reduced, Hoddesdon UDC gave the go ahead for the project.

THE OLD MILL

On the site to the south of the Coffin Houses in the late 1500s was a windmill or malt-mill which belonged to South Field to the east and next to it, opposite Cock Lane, was a track leading down to the common meads. An odd little building was erected on the side of Yew Arbour to serve as Hoddesdon UDC's office from 1894 to 1926 so that its first Clerk, Mr McKenzie, only had to pop next door to work. Later it became a newsagent, before serving as a hairdressing salon prior to being knocked down with its next door neighbours.

YEW HOUSE currently Cedar Green

Originally an ancient manor called Willifetts and later Sewalls which, by 1500, was the also the site of a row of houses - one of which was called 'The Rose'. These were bought by Lord Burghley in the late 16th century and let to John Borrell, landlord of the Star at the north end of the High Street, for a rent of a *'gilliflower'* for one, 1d per year for another, whilst the third was rented at *'a peppercorn'*.

A large house was built in the early 17th century at the time the estate was rented to John Bayley by Sir Robert Cecil. Tregelles tells us, *"There is in the kitchen garden of Yew House a curious well, known as Tinkers Well. It seems to have a supply pipe from Rawdon House and as the brickwork, which has good architectural features, is of that period, it probably belongs to the time of John Bayley's occupation. It was formerly used by the public and approached by Tinkers Lane."*

In the 1770s the mansion housed a girl's school run by a Mrs Tutty, and by 1790 it was the home of Edward Christian who taught at the East India

Demolition of Yew House (1962)

College at Haileybury. His brother was the notorious Fletcher Christian who led the mutiny on the Bounty in 1789. During the next century two Admirals lived there: Peere Williams and Donat Henchy O'Brien. The latter, who served bravely in the Napoleonic Wars and subsequently reached the rank of Rear-Admiral, gave his name to the lane nearby which is still known today as Admiral's Walk.

Land adjacent was sold in 1904 and the very exclusive Yewlands Estate was built along the south side. The house was demolished in 1962 and a whole cul-de-sac of new properties built on the site which was called Cedar Green. However, the stable block survived and was re-named North and South House which we can see over to the right today.

YEWLANDS HOUSE

If we gaze down Yewlands in front of us we can see the most impressive property to be built on the new estate just after the turn of the 20th century. It was specially designed by a leading London architect for Mr John Burton on a prime site which had the New River flowing along its eastern border. On the ground floor were a large entrance hall, dining room, drawing room and billiard room. Upstairs there were six bedrooms and a playroom. To one side of the property there was a pony box, but also a garage for the recently invented motor car.

In 1911 architectural drawings and both internal and external photographs

Yewlands (1911)

featured in *The Architectural Review* along with a description of the house. *"The materials are unpicked red brick facings, cream coloured rough cast, and hand-made tiles. The half-timber porch with brick noggin is solidly built of English oak, and the hall and staircase are oak panelled. The principal rooms have oak floors and purpose-made mantelpieces, while the ceilings have cast plaster ornamentation on the beams and as borders."*

HARTSHORNE

On the north corner of Upper Marsh Lane this historic house was originally a small inn known as 'Lez Harteshorne' belonging to the Tebbes family - this had been re-named the Five Bells by 1680. It was later known as 'South End House', but reverted to its original name under the occupancy of Colonel E J Christie of the brewing family.

THE ITALIAN COTTAGE currently THE SPINNING WHEEL

If we carefully cross the road our eye is now drawn down the green vista before us at the end of which is a charming and unusual villa built by John Warner's son Septimus in 1870 that became known as the 'Italian Cottage'. In the 1890s Septimus and his son Howard Low Warner were both living here. Some time in the early 20th century the building was sold and a road house called the Spinning Wheel was established, which became a popular stop for Edwardian travellers. It was a particular draw for those enjoying the new craze for cycling which bought thousands of Londoners out into the countryside.

In the 1930s a small, privately owned pool opened at the Spinning Wheel which required membership, *(page 112)*, leaving members of the Hoddesdon Swimming Club (in existence since 1895) to use the river at Dobbs Weir. However, Hertfordshire County Council paid for 300 pupils at local schools to visit the private pool on a weekly basis at the cost of 1d per visit per child. Mollie Muetzel enjoyed the facilities there. *"When I was at Broxbourne School we used to walk all the way through to learn to swim at the Spinning Wheel. And it was a lovely bit of pool there."*

In 1935 the people of Hoddesdon started to lobby Hoddesdon UDC to build a new swimming baths for the town to replace the pool at Christie's Brewery which had been lost when the complex was demolished. *(see page 123)* By September 1937, the *'Swimming Bath Controversy'*, as the *Hoddesdon Journal* called it, had reached such a pitch that the Hoddesdon & District Ratepayers' & Residents' Association held an open debate at St Cuthbert's Hall.

The Spinning Wheel (c1900)

Councillors at the meeting were worried about estimated costs leading to an increase in rates, while local residents argued that most nearby towns had already built public pools and that therefore Hoddesdon needed its own. One speaker with grandchildren insisted: *"Every facility should be provided for the young folk in order that they might keep fit. Our amenities have stood still while the population has doubled."*

The people of Hoddesdon had to wait another 12 years to get their municipal swimming baths – when Hoddesdon UDC finally agreed to purchase the very basic pool at the Spinning Wheel. The *Hoddesdon Journal*'s reporter was at Official Opening in May 1949. *"'It is not expected that this pool will pay big dividends in cash, but we do expect it will pay big dividends in happiness,' said Councillor R Gilling of Hoddesdon Council ... Councillor Fern said it was important that every boy and girl should learn to swim and recounted the benefits to be gained by such knowledge from the points of view of health, enjoyment and physical safety."*

Schoolboy Hedley Eariss wasn't very impressed. *"It always seemed freezing cold. The teaching methods there, now would be frowned upon I think, compared to how swimming is taught these days. It was very rough and ready. And then the changing facilities again, were very basic. I don't even recall there being showers at the time we were children."* Alan Cook has fonder memories. *"When you finished there was the little caravan on site where they served snacks and that sort of thing. And I always*

Official opening of the Open Air Swimming Pool (May 1949)

remember the lady in there, she sold peanut butter sandwiches which I loved - her name was Mrs Jennings." Over the winter of 1954 the facility was closed for improvements including larger changing rooms and more toilets, and the pool was extended to 25 yards to comply with Amateur Swimming Association rules.

When a new heated indoor pool opened in the 1980s at Broxbourne Lido, and another at John Warner School in 2002, the old open air pool was allowed to go into terminal decline by Broxbourne Council. When its closure was announced in 2010 there was concerted, vociferous and well-supported local campaign to save the facility, which sadly failed. The pool was demolished in early 2012. As Mollie Muetzel puts it so pithily: *"They've just closed it, I do believe. Isn't that a shame? Why do they improve everything and make it worse? Money, money, money."* Broxbourne Council have created the Diamond Jubilee Memorial Gardens with no recreational facilities on the pool site which, unsurprisingly, remain largely unused.

We now have to gird our loins to cross back over the busy A1170 without the aid of a pedestrian crossing for the final leg of our journey. On the opposite side we find ourselves examining one of the most unappealing examples of 1960s architecture: Hoddesdon Police Station.

An ariel view of the south of the town showing the new Council Offices (left), Elm Place (top centre), Lowewood (centre) and (bottom right) Woodlands (c late 1930s)

WOODLANDS

Originally known as Bradshaws in the 15th century and owned by the Rich family, Tregelles explains: *"this property, which was held by Francis Lucy of the Broxbournebury family in 1684, was re-named Woodlands when Mr John Warner built the present house, laid out the grounds with much taste, and made good use of the springs which break out on the hillside opposite."*

John Warner was born in 1776 into a wealthy family of Quakers who owned a metal foundry in the City of London. At the age of 14 he started as an apprentice in the family business and in 1798 he was admitted as a Freeman of the Worshipful Company of Founders. His long association with Hoddesdon started in 1802 when he married Esther Borham, the daughter of another wealthy Quaker family who lived in the town. Their first child George Borham was born in 1803 but died in infancy, although a daughter Anna and another son named John followed in 1804 and 1806.

However, the family was hit by a terrible tragedy in 1807 when Esther, pregnant with her fourth child, was brutally murdered while visiting her parents' home. *(see page 186)* In a tradition common in Victorian times, John married Esther's 21 year old sister Sarah four years later and they went on to have eleven children in a marriage that lasted forty years.

When his father died in 1816 John took over the running of the foundry. The company had started manufacturing bells in 1788 and John expanded the business with bells inscribed '*John Warner & Sons, London*' being made for churches all over England and exported across the world for the next 150 years. In 1834 John had the honour of being elected Master of the Founders Company, and by the time of his death the company had been given a Royal Warrant as Bell Makers by Queen Victoria and were operating works in Cripplegate, other locations in London and at the Norton Ironworks at Stockton on Tees.

A few years after John's death in 1851, the company won the hugely prestigious commission to cast the Big Ben bell for the newly built Houses of Parliament, along with the four quarter bells to chime every 15 minutes. Big Ben was designed as the largest bell ever made up to that time, which caused major problems. Once the enormous bell had been cast in Stockton it had to be transported down to London by sea on a ship which nearly sank. It was hung on a scaffold and tested daily until, to everyone's horror, it cracked and the John Warner & Sons' estimate for recasting it was rejected by the Government as too expensive.

Print showing the Quarter Bells by the John Warner Foundry (c1860s)

Another bell was hurriedly produced by the rival Whitechapel Foundry in London and rushed into place in the tower. When it was tested in position exactly the same thing happened with a large fracture appearing in the side. It took nearly three years for it to be repaired in situ, and the distinctive chimes we hear today are from that same damaged bell. But the quarter bells, which were completed by the John Warner Company in 1857 at the huge cost of £1840, are still those which ring out every 15 minutes between the hours to this day.

In the 1830s John, who was by now enormously wealthy, purchased this large area of land here on the west side of the main road at the south end of town to construct a large, double-fronted mansion he called Woodlands. At the south end of the property facing the main road at Spitalbrook there were several Gothic style cottages for the estate workers, also known as 'Braithwaite's Castle'. The 1851 census lists their tenants as 54 year old Head Gardner, James Williams along with his wife Sarah, 16 year old son Thomas (described as a labourer), and 14 year old daughter Hannah. Next door is elder son Benjamin Williams with his wife and 3 year old daughter, and a third cottage is the home of estate carpenter John Clark with his wife Mary who works as laundress and 10 year old cousin Louise who is a 'scholar'.

The Gothic Cottages (c1890s)

Woodlands from the park (c1890s)

In 1926 John Warner's 83 year old grandson, Metford Warner, wrote a fascinating childhood memoir of Woodlands and the surrounding estate entitled '*In My Grandfather's Time*'. Remembering his family's regular visits from London he describes the house as: *"somewhat uninviting in appearance with its white stucco front standing back from the footpath... the interest outside the house was in the big semi-circular brass knocker which, when used, came down with a thud... I do not think we had to use it, a watch no doubt being kept by the Aunts for our arrival and possibly one of them peeping from the dining room window on to the road through the little dwarf vertical venetian-like blind which closed and opened according to the turning of the knob at the top of the blind frame."*

The entrance hall was rather small, with the parlour or 'business room' to the right and the dining room to the left which adjoined the drawing room. In an adjacent corner was a canary aviary kept by Metford's Aunt Celia which had a painted background of tropical plants and birds. A glass door opened from the drawing room into the conservatory *"with its little fountain, citron tree in fruit, camellias, and choice flowering plants."* Upstairs was a small lobby full of anti-slavery water colour paintings by J B Campion which led through to John Warner's Library.

Metford has vivid memories as a small boy of *"the kitchen domain with its red tiled floor and the code of instructions for male and female servants painted on the wall or blackboard. Just beyond was the door to grandmother's storeroom, redolent of freshly baked seed cake, and tarts,*

The entrance hall at Woodlands (1938)

and those choice biscuits in the form of the figure eight encrusted with coriander seeds, and beyond all with the perfume from the freshly cut citrons now waiting to be turned into marmalade."

But the real glory of the property were the extensive gardens created by John Warner with the help of local landscape gardening firm Pulhams of Broxbourne and his Head Gardener, James Williams. Metford enthuses: *"My grandfather would not have claimed that he was an Artist, yet he must have been one at heart, otherwise he would not have converted an estate of some 30 acres of field and trickling stream into a garden of delight and surprises with its terraces, fountains, pools, fish ponds and summer-houses in each favoured spot."*

There were a series of inter-linking garden areas with different themes and several photos survive which show some of their statues, fountains and other decorative features. The estate had its own kitchen garden, rose garden, pinetum, lake and even a Roman-style bathhouse.

John Warner's own foundry supplied the extensive network of pipes and plumbing which James Pulham and his staff laid before creating the water features, ponds, lawns, borders and rockeries using their own manufactured 'pulhamite' stone. A London Guidebook published in 1851 enthuses about the gardens: *"there the spectator is astonished by the admirable imitation of broken rocks formed entirely of bricks and mortar which have all the appearance of having been worn by the current of the stream."*

Metford also tells us that his father's *"hobby and delight was in the cultivation of orchids."* These exotic blooms were only just arriving in England around this time and a special heated house was built in the grounds of Woodlands to accommodate them. Benjamin Williams was in charge of these rare plants and in later years became famous in gardening circles as the author of various books on the cultivation of ferns and orchids. The Warner blooms were regularly entered for the Chiswick and Regents Park Flower Shows.

Head Gardner James Williams had come to work for the family at the age of 18 and, according to Metford, remained with them until the remarkable age of 91 *"contented and happy with the work of his hands, tending his vines... and watching with loving care those many trees, shrubs and plants which he had planted in early days & taking an interest in the family to the 4th generation!"*

After John's death his wife remained in residence and was joined by her son, John Borham Warner, and his wife Elizabeth who had been married since 1835 with four surviving children, including Metford. Mary moved to live next door at Lowewood with her other single sister Celia.

By the late 1890s the house was listed as the home of Mrs Snow. Mr J A Hillyer was the owner from 1919 until his death in 1938 when the property was sold at auction as '*a comfortable Georgian residence*' with seven bedrooms, three reception rooms, a billiard room in nearly 12 acres of '*delightful old world gardens and grounds, lakes and parklands.*' Subsequently the ground floor of the property was used as offices for Hoddesdon Urban District Council and the upper floor was converted into flats. In 1967 the whole mansion was pulled down to make way for the new Hoddesdon Police Station.

Today the only remaining traces of the extensive Woodlands estate are the stable block and Orangery, both now converted into private homes and tucked away behind the unsightly police station block – the latter, in my opinion, being one of the hidden gems of our town. *(see page 118)* Metford Warner describes the Orangery as *"a lofty conservatory of sufficient length to take the orange trees of some 20ft high, standing in tubs, now rich with fruit and flower; the end wall treated as a recess to take an aviary with its background of painted tropical foliage and birds."*

The gardens at Woodlands with statues (c1890s)

According to him *"the stable yard is presided over by our great friend Henry the Coachman – that Henry who has been accustomed to drive our grandfather in his carriage and pair to and from his factory at Jewin Crescent (he never went by rail)... The beloved Henry welcomes us and takes us to see the carriage horses in the stable and 'Norway' (the Norwegian pony with hog mane)... Then we have a word with 'Nelson' (known to us as 'plum pudding'), the spotted Dalmatian hound with bloodshot eye who follows underneath or bounds at the side of the carriage when they go out in state."*

LOWEWOOD

Just next door we find this fine Georgian house intact, built around 1750 on land known as Harveys in the 17th century, later the home of the three unmarried daughters of John Warner: Harriette, Celia and Mary. According to Hayllar, the latter *"was a real type of earlier Quaker ladies. I can just remember her as she was in my boyhood and recall how she used at times the old Quaker forms of speech 'thee' and 'thou', 'first day', 'second day', etc, for the days of the week."* Mary is buried in Lord Street behind the Friends Meeting House along with many other members of her family and the Borhams.

By the mid 1930s there was heated public debate in the town about the lack of library facilities. Letters such as these began appearing regularly in the *Hoddesdon Journal*: *"Dear Sir, the present position of Library facilities in Hoddesdon in connection with the County Library is very unsatisfactory. Books are provided on one evening of the week only and no shelving accommodation is available, choice of reading is consequently very limited."* In 1936 the owner of Lowewood, Douglas Taylor, very generously gave his house to the town to be used as its first public Library.

One of the first tasks was for a part time Librarian to be recruited – the job went to Edward Paddick, who had just been forced bring his young family back to his home town from Canada as a result of the Great Depression. His daughter Olive Knight remembers what happened. *"Things were very hard for my father when we got back to England, and he did all sorts of odd jobs: gardening and he had a job for a short time at the Road House - the Spinning Wheel - and the Post Office... And he was at the Post Office when he was told that the Library was going to be opening in Hoddesdon, which interested him a lot."*

"He applied for the job and got it when he was 38. And never looked back really - he thoroughly enjoyed the work. And, of course, he was interested in anything to do with Hoddesdon - very interested in anything old. So he gathered together bits and pieces people brought him, bits of old Hoddesdon and that sort of thing and he eventually wrote a book."

The *Journal*'s man attended the Library opening: *"When Major O F Christie in his official capacity turned the key in the lock of the new public library at Lowewood on July 29th he opened up a path to wisdom and pleasure which today, and in the years to come, Hoddesdon people will tread to their advantage... The time may not be far distant when the Library will be open all hours of the day."*

Annette Marples used to go in there on a Saturday morning to *"choose my books that I wanted, but it was a case of being seen and not heard, like libraries used to be. If you were talking to people you'd be shushed because people were studying."* Hedley Eariss loved the garden out the back: *"I remember the big fishpond round the back, and the cage of budgerigars. I remember mother taking me up there just to see those, before I got a bit older and went into the building and the books."*

In 1952 the *Hoddesdon Journal* reported that *"Mr E W Paddick, the local Librarian, has been appointed by the Hoddesdon UDC as the honorary Curator of Records. In the future when a local historian decides to write a further history of Hoddesdon it will be from old documents, deeds, letters,*

Edward Paddick appointed as Honorary Curator of Records (1952)

that it will be compiled." Mr Paddick handed over his own extensive collection of documents, photos, ephemera and artefacts relating to his beloved home town in 1960. Although he retired as Librarian in 1963, he remained curator of the Record Room until 2 years before he died in 1976.

In 1977, when the new purpose-built Library was completed up in the town centre leaving Lowewood empty, plans by Broxbourne Council to sell off the historic building were scotched by the efforts of the Hoddesdon Society. The collection which had been so carefully built up and conserved by Edward Paddick over his lifetime now found a permanent home in a new museum created there in 1982 to serve the whole Borough.

BORHAM HOUSE

Where today we find another utilitarian 1960s structure, this one housing an NHS clinic, before 1965 we'd have been looking at a rather attractive period cottage. *(see page 188)* However, this innocuous property was the scene of a violent and bloody double murder back at the beginning of the 19th century, bringing tragedy to the wealthy Warners.

On Tuesday 20th October 1807 John Warner's first wife Hester, who was pregnant with their fourth child, was on a visit to her elderly parents, Mr and Mrs Borham. The family were enjoying a pleasant evening at home in the company of Mrs Hummerstone, housekeeper of the Black Lion Inn (now the Salisbury), when a recently-dismissed servant, Thomas Simmons, forced his way into the house. According to a contemporary account: *"this young man, it seems, had, while in the family, paid his advances to the servant Elizabeth Harris, who was many years older than himself, but the symptoms of a ferocious and ungovernable temper, which had frequently displayed, had induced his mistress to dissuade the woman from any connection with him, and his violent disposition had led also to his dismissal from this family."*

Armed with a knife, Simmons threatened Elizabeth Harris who locked herself in the scullery. At this point he was confronted by Mrs Hummerstone who had appeared at the back door, *"and with his knife stabbed her in the jugular artery, and pulling the knife forward, laid open her throat on the left side."* Rushing into the parlour the first person the murderer encountered was Mrs Warner *"and without giving her time to rise from her chair, he gave her so many jabs in the jugular vein and about her neck and breast, that she fell from her chair, covered with streams of blood, and expired."*

By this time Elizabeth had appeared having heard screams, and was in turn attacked by Simmons who, according to her trial evidence, threw her

A contemporary print of the Borham House Murder (1808)

to the ground and *"drew a knife across her throat, but she guarded it with her hand, which was cut. He made a second blow, when she wrested the knife out of his hand."* Simmons fled the scene, later telling the local constable that he'd been frightened off by an angelic intervention: *"when he had got Betsy down, he heard something fluttering over his shoulders, which made him get up and run away."* He was found about 100 yards away in a farmyard crib by Thomas Copperwheat and *"brought to the Bell alehouse where he was bound and handcuffed til morning."*

His subsequent trail at Hertford on 4th March 1808 caused a sensation; the Court House *"was uncommonly crowded with vast numbers from London, persons who had knowledge of the different parties, and many from adjacent villages."* Simmons was only tried for the murder of Mrs Hummerstone, as the Borham family refused to give evidence for the murder of their daughter due to their Quaker beliefs.

The proceedings were pretty straightforward as the witness had already confessed to several witnesses, and so the Jury pronounced Simmons 'guilty'. *"The Learned Judge with his usual formality proceeded to pronounce the awful sentence, which was to be hanged on Monday next, and his body to be anatomised. He heard the sentence with great indifference and walked coolly from the bar."*

Borham House (early 1960s)

ELM PLACE

After the terrible tale we've just heard let's swiftly turn to look to our right where there was another period property that we can no longer view.

Tregelles tells us, having lived at Elm Place in the 1890s, it was *"mostly built in the seventeenth or late 16th century, still showing the staples where its sign, 'The Dolphin' used to hang at the front. Like the other old inns, it brewed its own beer, and remains of the apparatus for this purpose were here until quite lately... Elm Place was doubtless named from two fine elms which stood there, one on each side of the highway and formed, as it were, a portal to the town."* It was later divided into two separate dwellings and early in the 20th century it was the residence of Mrs. Baskerville, Mrs. Hannah Hoskins and Miss Pinn. The house was demolished in 1965.

HODDESDON UDC OFFICES

We move on northwards across the road that now leads down to Broxbourne Civic Hall to see a rather imposing civic building which has survived into the 21st century. Due to the significant enlargement of Hoddesdon Urban District Council in the mid 1930s it was decided that the old offices at 60-62 High Street *(see page 162)* were not big enough, so this grand new Headquarters was built and officially opened on 21st December 1935 by then Chairman of the Council, R W Merchant. When the new Borough of Broxbourne was created in 1974 their offices were based down in Cheshunt and with the expansion of the Bishops College

A meeting of the Hoddesdon UDC in the Council Chamber (1950s)

site in 1986 this building was sold off and has since been successfully extended and adapted as sheltered accommodation for older residents.

THE GRANGE (15, High Street) currently Cedar Park Nursery

Carefully moving on to cross Cock Lane we come to the original site of the Cock Inn, where a dwelling was built around 1500. It was purchased in 1591 by William Thorowgood whose granddaughter became Dame Elizabeth Rawdon, and was added to the Rawdon estate as part of her marriage dowry in 1611. Her second son Marmaduke settled there after returning from his overseas travels in 1656 where *"he built a faire brick house provided with ponds, fountains, gardens, orchards, groves, wilderness and something of those curiosities that belong to a noble house."*

By 1725 it was owned by Lady Arabella Oxendon, daughter of the Second Baron Rockingham, who carried out improvements and alterations, as described by Tregelles. *"She also put in a new and, even for that day of fine woodwork, a handsome staircase with much carved oak about it, also a carved oak cornice in the study, and probably built the south wing, containing a new kitchen and other offices. The chief item of beauty added by Lady Arabella is the gateway at the end of the avenue, with its perfectly finished rubbed and moulded brick piers and elaborate wrought ironwork."*

Those same grand gates still stand opposite Barclay Park at what was once the end of the Grange's garden. In 1854 the mansion became a boy's Preparatory School run by Mrs Faithfull and her son-in-law Rev C G Chitterden. Prime Minister, A J Balfour, was educated there – we can still see his initials today carved into one of the bricks of the gates. By the early 1900s the property was owned Douglas Jones. Edward Paddick reminisces: *"Many older people of the town will remember with pleasure the Sunday School treats held in the grounds at the beginning of this century, and the picnic teas enjoyed in the meadow below the house."*

Tim Turner's family were friends of the owner in the 1950s. *"We knew Mrs Lorna Tuke Taylor well. She used to come to us for Christmas lunch. We sometimes visited her, but the house was cold and draughty and slightly scary! She was knocked over on the crossing by the (then) new Catholic Church of St Augustine. She died soon after and my mother joined a number of people who helped clear out the house."*

Local auctioneers were instructed to sell the contents of the house but just before the sale, the house was burgled and several of the lots were stolen. The sale took place on Wednesday 24 July 1968 when Tim was just 13 years old. *"There were 414 lots which totalled £12,000. There were several large Chinese vases and other Oriental items from the family's time in the East... the top price of the day was £750 paid for a painting of a naval engagement. We bought a lot described as 'a quantity of pictures'. This turned out to be a room full! We carted all of these back to our house at the bottom of Yewlands in a four wheel garden cart."*

The large garden of the property was then sold off for the construction of a housing estate, cleverly contained within the original garden walls, while the house itself changed ownership a number of times before becoming a private nursery school.

THE COTTAGE (19, High Street) currently Curwens Solicitors

Originally the site of the Birdbolt Inn, in last part of the 19th century this charming house had become a private school called 'The Middle Class Academy' run by Mrs Pratt. Mr Hayllar received his education there *"and a very good one it was, too."* In the post-war period it became the offices of Paul Wallace Estate Agents and today houses a solicitor's practice.

SHERBOURNE HOUSE

And so we finally find ourselves back where we began this trip – outside the garage. Only, before we say farewell, we need to focus on the left hand section of the forecourt where, just over half a century ago, we'd have seen a long, narrow 18th century mansion. Tregelles identifies this as *"Sherbourne House, which was built in 1760, stands on the site of a small house owned in 1573 by J Mitchell, a wealthy butcher, and adjoining it to the north stood 'The Stone House', not an inn and once known as 'Fullers'."*

In the late 1890s this was a private home occupied by Mr Ernest Beck. By the mid 1950s it had become a private club which advertised for members in the *Hoddesdon Journal*. That same publication reported the decision by the Hoddesdon UDC in November 1964 to allow for the demolition of the property - despite objections from the Ministry of Housing and Local Government and the Georgian Society on the grounds it was included in the Statutory List of Buildings of Special Architectural or Historical Interest. It was knocked down in 1965 during the expansion and re-development of the Hoddesdon Motor Company's premises.

CONCLUSION

And so here we are, having walked probably not much more than a mile and yet we've learned the history of more than 100 properties past and present dating back nearly 1000 years; met so many interesting people of many ages, backgrounds and classes; and seen Hoddesdon transformed by the ebb and flow of the tides of history from a tiny rural hamlet to a thriving 21st century community. We tend to think that constant change is either the blessing or curse, (according to our outlook), of the present age, but if we look at the conclusions of previous historians who have written about the town we find they were equally concerned about the transforming effect that outside forces might have on its future.

In his 1908 book Tregelles is clearly pessimistic about what could happen in the years ahead. *"Milling is extinct, as also are weaving, fulling, dyeing and tanning; factories slowly creep up the Lee Valley, attracted by the ease of water carriage, and it is hard to say how long it may be before we shall be invaded by large buildings with lofty chimney shafts, ousting the rural character which has been the privilege of the place since history began."*

Mr Hayllar, who had witnessed not one but two world wars, was plagued by similar doubts in 1948. *"Will the wheel of time, which has seen our town once but a hamlet, then an independent district, see it become just a unit in an ever-enlarging London, or will it retain its old individuality..? It would seem that more developments are foreshadowed, which might even end in Hoddesdon being amalgamated with one or other of the neighbouring districts. This, I feel sure, would meet with very strong local opposition."*

While the former was right about lofty chimney stacks being built – at least they are confined to a single power station with its three aluminium towers located well outside the town centre – his vision of a pastoral haven ruined by industrial blight has not come to pass due to the rigorous application of contemporary zoning regulations. Although I'm sure he would have been horrified, both personally and professionally as an architect, about the damage inflicted on the fabric and heritage of the town during the last half century of 'modernisation' driven by the consumer revolution.

The latter's fears about amalgamation and the lack of autonomy that might ensue, have indeed come to pass with the radical re-structuring of local government in the 1970s which created the bastard Borough of Broxbourne from a shotgun marriage between two fiercely independent local authorities. Whilst there certainly was local opposition to the reform, the ruthless logic of administrative economies of scale was imposed on every part of the country and is today seen as inevitable. And some people argue that the location of the local authority's HQ down in Cheshunt and their obsession with expanding Brookfield Farm over the last three decades has definitely been to the detriment of Hoddesdon.

But the old chemist's worries about his town being engulfed by the ever-expanding Capital have not yet come to pass, and one of the great pleasures of living in this area is the way in which it has retained its rural character whilst providing fast and efficient commuter access into the heart of London. This has, in large part, been prevented by the rigorous imposition of a 'green belt' policy to contain urban expansion on the fringes of London.

But this bulwark is under serious threat in the current political climate, and Hoddesdon finds itself in the front line, with a development of over 500 homes to be built on green belt land to the east of the town which has just been given approval by Broxbourne Council. High Leigh Garden Village will be the largest development seen in Hoddesdon in almost half a century, and sets a dangerous precedent for further erosion of the green belt.

In 1975 Edward Paddick wrote a scathing critique of the impact of 20th century planners and developers on the fabric of his own beloved town and thousands of others all over England under the title '*The Rape of Hoddesdon*'. His arguments make sobering reading even today. *"The fate of our town seems to be in the hands of a group of planners and developers, all apparently obsessed by the rectangular container, and trained to think that all deviation from the low common mean must be studiously avoided... the planners (appear to) want to get rid of all that is good, so that those who follow us are not able to make the comparison between what we once had, and the objects of unspeakable dullness they have erected."*

Crystal ball gazing is a very dangerous temptation for any historian, and it is a trap I will not be falling into. All I would observe is that it is up to the residents of a town to determine what kind of place they live in – and that means at times they have to take the trouble to stand up and fight local authorities, politicians, planners and other so-called 'experts' who think they know better than the rest of us. Democracy is a precious thing, and it is only by exercising it that it will stay strong and healthy.

Mr Paddick emphatically agreed: *"The steady spoliation of a town like Hoddesdon is, to those that knew it a generation ago, a sight so melancholy as to make one doubt the sanity of those who allow it to continue, and that means all of us who do nothing to arrest its insidious advance."* It is not the result of what people **say**, but what they are willing to **do** about it, which will ultimately determine the kind of neighbourhood and society we will all find ourselves living in tomorrow.

Edward Paddick deserves to have the final word: *"We shall be beyond hope if we ever reach the stage of being unable or unwilling to recognise that beauty has an imponderable value; can it be poetic nonsense to suggest that there may be some extra value in a shop, a church, or a home built with charm and beauty? Did not Ruskin say* **'A nation is only worthy of the soil and scenes that it has inherited, when by all its acts it is making them more lovely for its children'***.*"

HODDESDON IN WORLD WAR TWO

At the outbreak of hostilities on 3rd September 1939 the *Hoddesdon Journal* sombrely commented. *"And so we are at war, with right undoubtedly on our side, and although we may fear the conflict, we seem to be unanimous in thinking the war against the aggressor is now the only means of bringing peace to the grand old world. I wish to employ no exaggerated eloquence regarding the spirit in which Hoddesdon folk have accepted the situation, but it has certainly been wonderful to note the calm and cheerfulness which has been in evidence up to the time of writing. We can only hope that spirit will prevail throughout hostilities."*

Ironically what then followed was a period when nothing seemed to be happening – the so-called 'phoney war'. According to Peter Shepherd: *" I don't remember anybody being all that concerned about it at the time, perhaps we didn't realise what was going to happen later on, but at that time I don't think anyone was overly worried about it."* But during this time the whole landscape of the district began to change as the authorities got defences ready for a possible German invasion.

Michael Dear describes the local preparations. *"Well from Slipe Lane at Wormley, there was a line of concrete blocks which were, I suppose, about five foot square, about six foot high and there was about three or four feet between each block. At the High Road there was a pillbox which was brick built. And across the High Road they had these railway lines bent into a 'U' shape. They dug holes in the road, and they used to drop ten of these railway lines into the holes and then put barbed wire in front*

Hoddesdon High Street just before the outbreak of World War II

of those. And then tank traps went from there, right over to where Tesco now is - there was one massive tank trap across the butts and over the New River."

"*Of course, when the war started, it more or less set Hoddesdon alight*", says Arthur Wingate, who worked at the Post Office. "*Whereas you had just the regular local people, with only one or two on the counter, you had all these people evacuated - private individuals down Dobbs Weir and around all the shantytown places. They were all evacuated to Hoddesdon.*"

Families were encouraged to build their own private shelters. "*We dug our own shelter in our garden, under an enormous plum tree*", says Mary Newton.*" It had every convenience - except that it was damp and miserable. I used to do most of my homework in there. I can remember going down there regularly when sirens used to go at about half past six or seven. We used to troop down there, and emerge as the dawn was breaking. It was not a pleasant experience at all."*

At the start of the war the fear of gas attacks meant that the Government issued gas masks to every child and many civilians, which they were supposed to carry with them at all times in a cardboard box with a string handle. The *Journal* helpfully published a little ditty to remind everyone to keep their masks at hand.

O milkman at the break o' day,
O cowman as you plod your way,
And children when you go to play,
Take your gas mask.
O Baker as you knead your dough,
And hawker passing to and fro,
Hear my warning soft and slow,
"Take Your Gas Mask".

Whilst these precautions thankfully proved unnecessary, there was plenty of aerial activity in the skies above the town. Michael Dear and his mates used to climb up a tall water tower at Rochford's Nursery where there was an observation platform. "*If we looked over towards North Weald we could see the aircraft taking off so we knew when the sirens were going to go. Of course we had many dogfights - I remember one on a Saturday afternoon, there was a real heavy raid on North Weald and I think there was one or two aircraft went down in smoke and everybody was standing in back gardens clapping. I can hear my father saying: 'Oh, don't be so bloody silly. It might be one of ours!' It was that high you couldn't see.*"

Boys became avid plane spotters, as Peter Haynes recalls. *"We stood there sometimes in daylight watching the German airplanes coming over to London. We were so young, of course, we didn't realise the danger. And then there were the dog fights – it was the Mosquitoes coming up from Hunsdon aerodrome that were attacking the incoming enemy aircraft - and you'd often hear the planes coming down, and the noise of them diving down and crashing. It was quite exciting I suppose."* Peter Shepherd has similar memories of *"various planes whizzing around, you could hear the machines guns going, vapour trails and smoke trails and things like that. And of course when we got to know the type of plane that had been brought down - if a German one was brought down we cycled out to try and look at it and, if possible, steal pieces off of it."*

In 1940, and again towards the end of the war, bombs fell regularly around the vicinity. Figures compiled later reveal 341 high explosive and 4500 incendiary bombs were dropped in Hoddesdon District, leading to the remarkably small number of 6 deaths and 15 injuries. Olive Knight's home had a few near misses. *"The bombing at night brought down our ceilings in our flat and broke windows - that happened twice. And there were incendiary bombs, which didn't seem to do any damage, although in our garden there were the holes where they had come down. And, of course, there was the big one in Yewlands which was quite near to us."*

The *Hoddesdon Journal* reported obliquely on the terrible bombardment and loss of life during the Battle of Britain in October 1940, and paid homage to the indomitable spirit being displayed by Londoners. *"During the past month the districts around us have not escaped from the raider's 'frightfulness'. We have heard reports not of grouses, criticisms, panic or discord, but of commendable courage and calm acceptance of the situation. The injured have shown extreme fortitude, the homeless patience, the rescuers devotion to duty, and the onlooking public a ready appreciation of the efforts of the services. May it long continue thus."*

Every building was now expected to be completely blacked out so the German bombers could not see their targets clearly, as Michael describes. *"We had blackouts and things like that, cinemas closed. Well, all the streetlights would go out at twelve o'clock or if there was a raid the lights went out - the street lamps. Because we had shutters and thick curtains that went round every window."* But this precaution was often neglected during the phoney war period, as we can tell from the repeated reminders carried in the *Hoddesdon Journal*. 'Hoddesdon By Night' was a headline in September 1939 *'Ah, did you see that light break through the darkness? Someone's being careless. Whose window or door is that left uncovered? If you value the wellbeing of yourself and those around you, see that it is not **yours**.'*

Christmas as usual

Owing to the Black-out we are unable to light our windows, but if you are looking for a present FOR HIM, pay a visit to our Showroom, where we have a splendid selection of Gifts suitable for the TROOPS and CIVILIANS.

SHIRTS • PYJAMAS • GLOVES • TIES
HANDKERCHIEFS • WOOL COATS
SCARVES • SLIPOVERS • HOSIERY, Etc.
DRESSING GOWNS
TROUSER PRESSES
DAKS AND LAMBOURNE FLANNELS
FOR MEN AND WOMEN

CHURCH & SON
For Modern Men's Wear
91 High St., HODDESDON
Phone 2125

**If Hitler Won't Or Hitler Will
We'll Keep Our Christmas Merry Still**

Useful Christmas Gifts
Are the order of the day.
You will find them all at Bristow's
And there won't be much to pay.
Our windows will delight your eye
And sure to make you come and buy.

A FEW SUGGESTIONS

LADIES' HANDKERCHIEFS . TOWELS . BOLSTER SETS . MEN'S HANDKERCHIEFS
CUSHIONS . TABLE CENTRES . LADIES' HOSE . CUSHION COVERS . PETTICOATS
MEN'S HOSE . FANCY TABLECLOTHS . TEA COSIES . BED JACKETS . BED SOCKS
CHILDREN'S KNICKERS . UNDIE SETS . LADIES' KNICKERS . GLOVES . APRONS
NIGHTDRESSES . PILLOW CASES . OVERALLS . PYJAMAS . PLAIN TABLECLOTHS
NIGHTDRESS CASES . CORSETS . PINARETTES . DUCHESS SETS . LADIES' VESTS
TEA-CLOTHS . TABLE RUNNERS . CHILDREN'S VESTS . PRAM COVERS
MEN'S SHIRTS . MEN'S TIES . BABIES' DRESSES . ETC. ETC.

86 ERNEST BRISTOW 86
High Street - Hoddesdon

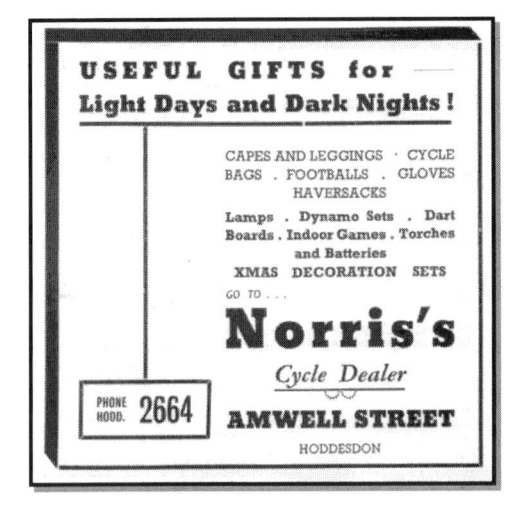

USEFUL GIFTS for Light Days and Dark Nights!

CAPES AND LEGGINGS . CYCLE BAGS . FOOTBALLS . GLOVES
HAVERSACKS
Lamps . Dynamo Sets . Dart Boards . Indoor Games . Torches and Batteries
XMAS DECORATION SETS

GO TO ...

Norris's
Cycle Dealer

PHONE HODD. **2664**

AMWELL STREET
HODDESDON

Hoddesdon Journal adverts Christmas 1939

The shops were faced with a real problem at Christmas 1939 as the black-out forbade them to illuminate their windows. Their adverts in the *Journal* reflect their different reactions. Bristows drapers had a rhyming riposte: '*If Hitler Won't or Hitler Will, We'll Keep Our Merry Christmas Still.*' Jeweller R C Saint declared emphatically: '*You Must Not Black-out Xmas.*' Norris's Cycles offered '*Useful gifts for Light Days and Dark Nights*'. The dry cleaners, Suitall, encouraged residents to embrace the new policy of 'make do and mend': '*WAR OR NO WAR we must keep clean and tidy, and our service can do this for you. Those OLD CLOTHES can be made quite good again thus saving NEW ONES at ten times the cost.*' It was left to dear old Gardiner's ironmongers to evoke the gung-ho spirit of the Great War. '*When the BLACK-OUT rush was on, people came from miles around because they knew they could get it from Gardiner's. We did not fail them. While our boys are giving Hitler a good grinding, let us grind your Lawn mower ready for peace next Spring!!*'

Most civilians who were left behind after the able-bodied men had been called up to fight were expected to help with all aspects of the defence of the home front. Mary Newton's uncle was in the Home Guard. "*It was just like 'Dad's Army'. They used to meet at 'Maggie's' - as we used to call the pub which was the William IV in Lord Street. And as children we used to love watching them after they'd had their parade on a Sunday morning. My uncle was like Corporal Jones - because he used to shoot at Bisley, he was the only one with a gun!*" Michael's father was an air raid warden, "*so, of course, we had to walk up the High Street and see if there were any lights shining. We had a whistle, you see. A whistle, and a rattle if there was gas.*"

Tommy Knight explains how veterans of the previous war like his father played a key role. "*Everyone took things in their stride really; if they were in town they did some sort of service - civil defence or something like that - some kind of service. My father was in charge of the Control Room underneath the Council Offices. He used to go out with Ralph Merchant ... and see where bombs had dropped and report them - unexploded bombs and so on.*" "*My father – 'wiggle' Haynes as he was known throughout his football career – he was in the Special Constabulary,*" Peter Haynes remembers, "*and his job when the sirens went was to jump on his bicycle and go down to Nissens at Rye House, and there was a very deep shelter there... And they used to look out for fires and bomb damage and things like that.*"

In December 1939 a public meeting was held by the British Legion at Esdaile Hall to set up the Hoddesdon & District Comforts Fund for '*the welfare of the Hoddesdon men serving in H M Forces*'. One of their first fund-raising efforts was a gala concert at the Pavilion Cinema which featured two major radio stars of the day - Rex Rodgers, the famous Irish Tenor presented the show, assisted by 'Radio's Own Comedienne', Suzette Tarri. The *Journal* reported on the success of the evening: *"the concert ran with pleasing continuity and smoothness, so that the minimum time was lost in that three and a half hours of delightful entertainment. Nearly a thousand people attended the concert and the proceeds, about £80, have passed to the British Legion's Cigarette and Comforts fund for the local 'boys' serving in France and on the seas."*

The Comforts Fund used the money it raised to send parcels of hand-knitted clothing such as gloves, scarves, balaclavas and other useful items including cigarettes to troops who came from the neighbourhood. Special Christmas Cards were printed featuring photographs of the town which people sent to re-assure their menfolk they were not forgotten. A NAAFI canteen was set up in Esdaile Hall where Mary Norton helped out. *"My aunt was a regular who went there and helped served food, and I used to go along and help her sometimes. It was something I'd never done before and I wasn't very old but it was very interesting. Yes - I felt I was doing my bit, even if it was only beans on toast!"*

Of course many local families suffered tragic losses, and Arthur Wingate and his colleagues at the Post Office increasingly found themselves the

Hoddesdon Journal advert for concert at the Pavilion Cinema (1939)

Christmas card produced by Comforts Fund (1943)

bearers of bad tidings. *"Sometimes the telegrams were very serious, when the messenger boy went out to deliver them we had to tell him 'that's reporting the death or injury of somebody, because the recipient is going to be really upset', so we had to warn the messenger boy about what might happen."*

As the war dragged on, rationing became more severe and privations increased but the civilian population continued to be encouraged to donate funds for the war effort. Like most other towns Hoddesdon had a Spitfire Fund, contributed to 'Battleship Week' and residents were regularly asked to invest their dwindling savings in War Bonds, as Arthur Wingate who worked at the Post Office recalls. *"I remember they had a big stall by the Clock Tower... I can't recollect what the figures were, but they certainly collected an awful lot of money with these war bonds. Everybody was terribly generous. It amazed me where all the money came from."*

And Michael Dear reminds us that people were expected to save and recycle everything possible while the country was being blockaded by the Nazi U Boats. *"We used to have a dustbin outside the front, or on the footpath, and you had one for chicken feed, and the other one for pig slop. We used to fill these dustbins up, and the council used to come round every Monday morning and collect the bins. Nothing went to waste. Yes, aluminium saucepans. Turnford Villas had all this lovely wrought iron*

Adverts for various fund-raising campaigns during World War II

fencing there, and of course they were all cut down and taken away - you know, melted down."

But, remarkably, Arthur Wingate confirms that civilian morale remained buoyant. *"It absolutely amazed me - because never, at any point, from the 3rd September 1939 onwards, did we ever think we'd lose the war. Even Dunkirk, we never thought we'd lose the war and everybody thought the same. It was just a question of how long before we would **win** the war. That was the general attitude of all the people."* Olive Knight agrees: *"I don't really remember any depression or people being miserable, everyone seemed to carry on with it pretty well really."*

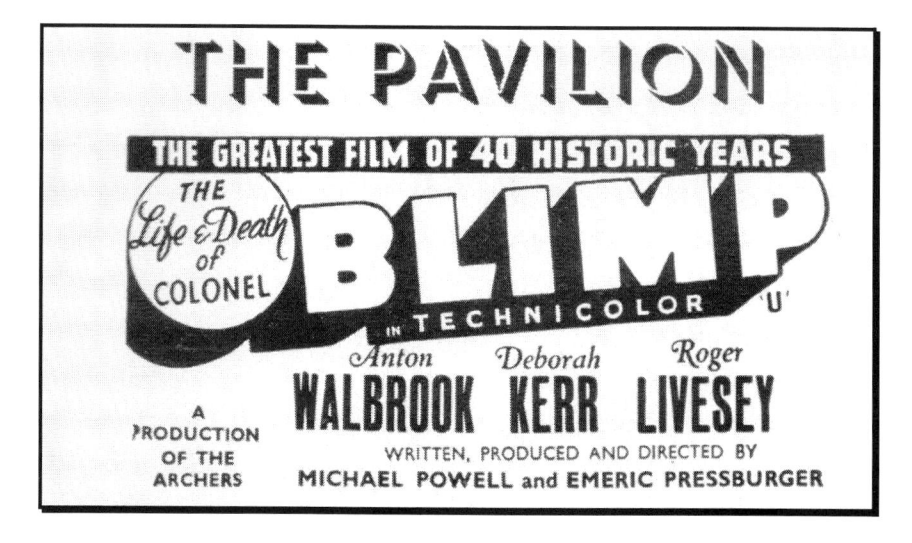

Films shown at the Pavilion Cinema during World War II

By 1944 the Allies were preparing to invade Europe and all sorts of new people began appearing, according to Arthur. *"There were troops everywhere, of course, before I was called up. I remember seeing the Americans, they'd arrived and they were around. Because at the time we had a couple of very attractive ladies at the counter, they attracted the Americans."* The new troops were a huge draw for kids like Michael Dear. *"I can remember just before D-Day, there were a lot of Americans and Canadians coming in convoys down the A10... stopped there overnight to do all their cooking with their fuel kitchens and baked tins of steak. They had stews and things to make in those days so, of course, we used to go round there - we used to get sugar and chewing gum."*

As the armies advanced across France pushing the Germans back towards the heart of the Reich, Peter Shepherd started to see other unfamiliar faces appearing. *"After D Day I remember seeing prisoners of war coming through the town from time to time. I remember a blue uniform with a big red spot on the back, I think. But you didn't really see that many of them, but they were around - German and Italian prisoners."* Many of these prisoners, especially the Italians, were put to work in the glasshouses that ran all the way down the Lea Valley.

When victory finally seemed imminent in 1945, despite all the privations of the previous six years, the people of Hoddesdon were more than ready

Audience at the 'Final Parade' in the Drill Hall (May 1945)

The 'Rivoli Revels' provide the 'fun' at the Final Parade (May 1945)

to celebrate. In May at the Drill Hall a 'Final Parade' was held to stand down the town's sizeable army of voluntary Civil Defence workers. Mr Haward, who had served as Leader of the Hoddesdon UDC for the duration, told the packed ranks that the comparative freedom from bombs in the district had largely been due to the rigorous enforcement of the blackout by local police and ARP wardens. He continued, *"when you commenced your training and began exercises in the street, many people looked upon those exercises as a form of free entertainment provided for their amusement. Later, when in the blackout, the German bombers droned overhead and the air was filled with the noise of gunfire and bursting shells to say nothing of falling shell splinters, those people were comforted by the reassurance that you were at your posts and that should bombs fall in the town you would be on the scene quickly."*

Mr Plumpton, the 'Controller' responsible for co-ordinating all the various civil defence forces during the previous five years, was presented with cufflinks and a propelling pencil amidst loud and sustained applause. In a speech he revealed that during his tenure of the post there had been 70 incidents in Hoddesdon involving twelve injuries and five deaths. Musical entertainment at the end of the evening was provided by the 'Rivoli Revels'.

Annette Marples has very happy memories of the party that took place at Rye Park when VE day finally arrived on 8th May. *"We had a big bonfire*

The Victory Parade through Hoddesdon High Street (May 13th 1945)

on Pound Close and I can remember all holding hands and dancing around this bonfire. Everyone was obviously very, very excited because the war had ended."

A Victory Parade through the High Street was organised on Sunday 13th May, followed by a Church Service outside at Lowfield. The *Hoddesdon Journal* wondered where all the flags and bunting which had suddenly appeared all over the town had come from. *"Considering that the opportunities for their use have been rare or brief for the past five of six years, it was amazing to see every house and cottage, every shop and factory, suddenly blossom out with some kind of victory symbol. It was a triumph of careful storage throughout the dark days, a proof of faith in ultimate victory which sustained the whole of the land, even when things looked their blackest... A happy aspect of the festivities was the complete absence of rowdiness or drunkenness throughout the period."*

As a culmination of the celebrations on 14th July 1945 the people of Hoddesdon gathered to enjoy a grand Victory Fete on the cricket field at Lowfield organised jointly by the British Legion and the Hoddesdon Comforts Fund.

Victory Fete at Lowfield (July 1945)

MAIN CONTRIBUTORS

John Allison
Born Hoddesdon 1952

Val Bateman
Local resident since 1951

Diana Borchards
Born Broxbourne 1935

Dorothy Chilton
Born Hoddesdon 1920

Alan Cook
Hoddesdon Resident since 1939

Evelyn Dellow
Hoddeson Resident since 1957

Michael Dear
Born Turnford 1933

George Don
Born Hoddesdon 1931

Hedley Eariss
Born Hoddesdon 1949

John Gervis
Worked in Hoddesdon from 1959

Peter Haynes
Born Hoddesdon 1935

Tommy Knight
Born Hoddesdon 1920

Olive Knight
Local Resident since 1933

Annette Marples
Born Hoddesdon 1940

Mollie Muetzel
Born Hoddesdon 1925

Mary Newton
Born Hoddesdon 1927

Malcolm Norris
Born Hoddesdon 1939

Cyril Phelps
Evacuated to Nazeing 1940

Les Riches
Hoddesdon Resident since 1947

Peter Shepherd
Born Hoddesdon 1929

William J Smith
Born Hoddesdon 1944

Neville Townsend
Born Broxbourne 1945

Richard Thomas
Hoddesdon resident since 1967

Tim Turner
Born Hoddesdon 1955

Joan Umney
Evacuated to Hoddesdon 1940

Brian Walsh
Born Broxbourne 1938

Tina Ward
Hoddesdon resident since 1924

Arthur Wingate
Born Hunsdon 1923

Mary Young
Born Hoddesdon 1935

Abbott Tailors 128-9
Achille Serre Dry Cleaners 27-8
Allen's Cycle & Wireless Store 15
Almshouses 135
Amwell Street 25,76,87-9,95,133
Arbon & Upton 26
Archer & Turners Grocers 25-6
Arthur William House 53
Ashfield's Estate Office 28
Ashford, Henry John 37,159
Ashford's Grocery Store 37-8
Ashleys Gifts 17
Barclays Bank 33
Barclay Park 65
Barclay, Robert 64-5,85
Batsford Fishmongers 155
Batstone Tailors 140,141
Baxter's Butchers 14,15
Beech Walk 64
Beehive Cafe 34-36,45
Bell Inn 103, 107-8, 188
Bell Lane 78,108,123
Big Ben 179-80
Birdbolt Inn 191
Blackeby's Shoe Shop 27
Black Lion Inn 71,188
Bobbies Boutique 151,155
Bombing 1941 14
Bond & Son Jewellers 25,112,134,135,
Book Centre 29-30
Borham, John 164
Borham House Murder 178, 186-8
Bradford & Bingley 29
Bradley's Gents Outfitters 62-3
Bradshaws 178
Brewery 78,122-125,150
Brewery House 127,128
Brewery Road 122,125-127
Brewster's Fishmongers 77,79,137,155
Bridgeman & Son 159

Brill's Fishmongers 155-6
Bristow Drapers 151
British Girls School 41-2
British Legion 24,167,169
British School for Boys 167
Brocket Road 29-33,46,121
Brocket Road Stores 31,32
Brook's Ironmongers 37,38
Brookfield Farm 152-4,193
Broxbourne Borough/Council 45,99,129,152-155,186,189,192-3
Carisbrook Laundry 49
Carnivals 105-6
Carter's Shoe Shop 49-53
Cathrow, George 122
Central Radio Stores 53,111
Charles I 9,169
Charles II 9
Chequers Inn 55
Christian, Edward 173
Christie, Charles A 66,74
Christie, Charles Peter 82,123-4,127,149,171
Church's Dress Shop 142
Church & Son Menswear 63
Clabours 25
Clarke's Grocers 134
Clement Clarke Opticians 76
Clement Grocers 28-9
Clock House 101-2
Clock House Garage 92-4
Clock Tower 91-2,102-7,111
Cock Inn 190
Cock Lane 190
Coffin Houses 172
Collings Stationers 33
Coleman's Shoes 161
Combat Stores 37
Complete Angler 9,128
Conduit Lane 131,147,151,155-6
Congregational Church 9
Co-operative Stores 33-4,37-39,151

Corner House 121
Cottage, The 88-9,191
Countryside Wools 54
Cousin's Toyshop 49,54,138
Crown & Mitre Inn 159
Dane Cleaners 121
Dawson Jewellers 25,
Dellow Bakery 26
Deste Photographic Studio 71
Dewhurst Butchers 128,129
Dexter, Ray 100,147-8
Dickinson's Printers 62
Doctors House 164-5
Dolphin Inn 56,190
Domesday Book 8,11
Down Hall 56,57
Drury Brothers 66
Dymock's Decorators 136-7
Easiephit 36
Eason's Drapers 53,55
Eastern Electricity Showroom 142
Edward I 9
Elizabeth I 9,92
Elizabeth II 104
Elizabeth's Florists 15,26,
Ellis, Sarah and William 41-2, 63-4,170
Elm Place 189
Ermine Street 8
Esdaile Hall 167-9
Esdaile House 166
Esdaile Lane 167
Esdale House 166
Evacuees 83,84
Excelsior Baker 71
Fair 118,132,133
Falcon on the Hoop 44
Fawkon Walk 30,42,43,107,116
Fire Engine 124
Floral Wise 79
Flower & Swift Estate Agents 75
Fordham & Co 75,76,119-121
Four Feathers Inn 108

Fox Inn 150-1
Frank Andrews Sadler 49
Frank Turner's Car Mart 6
Franklin, Tom 168
Friends Meeting House 63,185
Frogley, William 11
Gardiners Ironmongers 66,131, 141-2
Garniers Jewellers 36,
Gas Board 73,94
Gateways Supermarket 61
George Inn 42
Gibson's Barbers 155-6
Gibson Greengrocers 13-4,43
Giddings, Charles 150
Gocher's Butchers 44-6
Golden Lion 7,10
Golden Lion Garage 6
Gothic Cottages 180
Gowers shops 139-40
Grace's 65
Grange, The 190-1
Griffin Inn 44,49
Gurney Drapers 151
Hampton, William 14,30
Hare's Grocers 42,43,158
Hartshorne 175
Haward, Walter John 54,74,143-7,156
Hayllar's Pharmacy 18-21
Heathers Tobacconist 34-36,115
Heathers & Meadows 41,53
Heron Group 90-92,97
Hertfordshire Circulating Library 163-4
Hicklings Menswear 27,53
Hickman, Ron 32
High Leigh 64,65
High Leigh Garden Village 99, 193
High Path 25,77,87
Hitching's Shoe Shop 76
Hoddesdon Dairy 28
Hoddesdon Employment Exchange 32,37

210

Hoddesdon Forge 70
Hoddesdon Journal 125-127
Hoddesdon Library 142,185-6
Hoddesdon Motor Company 6,191
Hoddesdon Parish Church 64,80-3,153
Hoddesdon Players 167-8
Hoddesdon Post Office 37, 159-60
Hoddesdon Society 60-2,107, 152,186
Hoddesdon Swimming Club 78,124,175
Hoddesdon Urban District Council 15,60,66, 90-2,131,144, 150,161-2,172-3,175-6, 185, 189-90,193
Hoddesdon & Broxbourne Unionist Club 157
Hogges Hall 9,161
Holly Bush Inn 107
Home & Colonial 13-4
Howarth Footwear 161
Hunt, John Alfred 66,81,159, 161-2,171
Hunt Insurance Office 162
Hutchinson's Opticians 34
International Stores 14,15
James I 9,169-70
Johnson's Bakers 71
Jones, Rev William 57,122
Kucza Watch Repairs 31
Langham & Scott 48
Laurels The 11
Lea Carpets 158
Lewis & Hill Estate Agents 28
Lock, Edward W 15,66
London Central Meat Co 137-8
Long & Blundell 49
Lord Street 63-5,123,153
Lord Street Coffee Tavern 65,66,
Lovedays 112,162-3
Lowewood 150,184-6

Maidenhead Inn 92-3
Market 129-132
Market Cross 130,131
Market House 58,
Martin, Charlie 125-6
Mary Tudor 9
Mawson, Peter 8
McAdam, James Loudon 76, 160
McKenzie, Alexander 172-3
Meadows Delicatessen 39-41, 45, 78,96, 99,153-4
Meek's Giftware 15,54
Middle Row 130,131
Midland Bank 27
Millar Opticians 76
Milletts 37,75
Mitchells 26,27,67
Modern Stores 75
Montague House 160
Morrisons 100,117
Myddleton House 74-76,115
National Schools 85-7,144
Newman's Restaurant 150
Nicholl's Florists 163-4,113
Nicholl's Butchers 69,70
Nicholl's Greengrocer 37
Nicholl's Undertakers 54-5
Night Must Fall 110
Norris Drapers 15-8
Norris Bikes & Electrical 89-91, 95,100
Nuttall family 17
O'Brien, Donat Henchy 174
Oddfellows Society 57
Old Bakerie Shop 140-1
Old Harrow pub 77
Old North Road 8
Outdoor Swimming Pool 78, 156,175-6,175-7
Owen Chemists 75
Oxendon, Lady Arabella 191-2
Paddick, E W 60-1,99,172, 185-6,193-4
Parker's Bakery 22

Parrott Brothers 23
Paul's Lane 21,79-80,83,
85,87,108,144
Paul Wallace Estate Agent 87-9,
95,192
Pavilion Cinema 108-10
Peacock's Barbers 47,48
Pearce's Bakery 55,
Pearsons of Enfield 46
Pedestrianisation 41,151-5
Pepys, Samuel 9
Pevsner, Nikolaus 69,70,98-9,152
Phoenix Fire Office 54
Pigott's Omnibus 103
Plomer, Robert 80,122,170
Police Station 63,102,103,
177,184
Population 11
Porter's Needlework 161
Powells of Ware 55,
Pulhams of Broxbourne 182-3
Queens Head 74
Rathmore House 74,164-5
Rawdon House 62,157,169-72
Rawdon, Sir Marmaduke 44,58,
92,148,169-70
Reynolds Jewellers 66,71
Ricardo, Henry K 170-1
Ripley's Butchers 69,70
Robert's Hotel & Cafe 128
Rosehill 41,63-4
Ross's Forage Stores 77-8
Rumbelows 28,29
Rye House Plot 10
Sainsbury's supermarket 30,46,
St Augustine's Church 165-6,
190
St Katherine's Chapel 80,100-1,
164
St Monica's Priory 171-2
Saint's Jewellers 143
Salisbury Arms 10,71-3,131-3
Samaritan woman 148-50
Sams & Bryants 77

Seaton's Confectioners 49
Sharp's Chemist 158-9
Sherborne House 6,191
Shirley's Wool Shop 32
Shoe Box 53
Spinning Wheel 175-7
Stagg's Boot Shop 71,113,124,
135-6
Stallabrass Butchers 141
Stanboroughs 156-8
Star Inn 71,173
Stone's Radio & Electrical 113,
161
Suitall Valet Service 121
Symes Sports 150-1
Taplin Brothers 75
Taylor, Lorna Tuke 190
Teddar Barber 47
Tescos 41,99,100,133,154,
Thatched House Inn 128
Theobalds 9,170
Thomas Knight Printers
20,74,125-7,143
Thorowgood family 44,54,68,
92,169,190
Timothy Whites 12
Toc H 71
Tower Centre 90-2,94-100,
107,114,116,146
Town Pump 149
Tregelles, J A 159,
Tuck & Sinclair 159
Tudor Cafe 143,146
Tudor Hall 147-8
Tuke, Lucas & Seebohm Bank
33
Turnpikes 10
Union Society 57
Victoria Diamond Jubilee 64,
129,130
Victoria Wine 133
Vine Inn 10
Walker, Mike 152-5
Walton, Izaac 9,128
War Memorial 111,133-4

212

Ward's Newsagents 66-8,71
Ware Valley 76
Warner, John 41,63-4,167,170, 178-84,187
Warner, Howard L 66,175
Warner, Metford 63,181-5
Warner, Septimus 33,66,175
Wash & Son Grocers 37
Webb, Charles 64
West, Dr Leonard 165
Westminster Bank 139-40
White Heather Dairy 28
William Clark Printers 73
Williams Brothers 11-12
White Hart Inn 137

White Hinde 7
White Horse Inn 137
White Swan 68-70,139
Whiting's Antiques 160
Woodlands 118,178-85
Woolwich Building Society 25
Woolworths 12
Workmate 32,127
World War Two 195-207
Wyman & Son 27
Yew Arbour 172-3
Yew House 9,173-4
Yewlands House 174-5
Zavaroni, Lena 100
Zetters Bingo 110,115